A Martial Reader

BC **LATIN** Readers

Series Editor:
Ronnie Ancona

These readers provide well annotated Latin selections written by experts in the field, to be used as authoritative introductions to Latin authors, genres, topics, or themes for intermediate or advanced college Latin study. Their relatively small size (covering 500–600 lines) makes them ideal to use in combination. Each volume includes a comprehensive introduction, bibliography for further reading, Latin text with notes at the back, and complete vocabulary. Nineteen volumes are currently scheduled for publication; others are under consideration. Check our website for updates: www.BOLCHAZY.com.

A Martial Reader
Selections from the Epigrams

Craig Williams

Bolchazy-Carducci Publishers, Inc.
Mundelein, Illinois USA

Series Editor: Ronnie Ancona
Volume Editor: Laurie Haight Keenan
Contributing Editor: Timothy Beck
Cover Design & Typography: Adam Phillip Velez
Map: Mapping Specialists, Ltd.

A Martial Reader
Selections from the Epigrams

Craig Williams

Bolchazy-Carducci Publishers, Inc.
1570 Baskin Road
Mundelein, Illinois 60060
www.bolchazy.com

Printed in the United States of America
2011
by United Graphics

ISBN 978-0-86516-704-9

Library of Congress Cataloging-in-Publication Data

Williams, Craig A. (Craig Arthur), 1965-
  A Martial reader : selections from the epigrams / Craig Williams.
    p. cm. -- (BC Latin readers)
  Texts in Latin with introductory material and commentary in English.
  Summary: Latin selections from Roman poet Martial (Marcus Valerius Martialis), with
vocabulary and grammar notes. Includes an introduction, two maps, full vocabulary, and
selected bibliography.
  ISBN 978-0-86516-704-9 (pbk. : alk. paper) 1. Latin language--Readers--Poetry. 2.
Latin language--Grammar--Problems, exercises, etc. 3. Martial. Epigrammata--Problems,
exercises, etc. 4. Epigrams, Latin--Problems, exercises, etc. I. Martial. Epigrammata.
Selections. II. Title.
  PA2095.W53 2011
  878'.01--dc22

                                                                        2011005615

Contents

List of Illustrations

Preface

Generations of students of Latin have encountered Martial in bits and pieces—an epigram here, another there, scattered through textbooks by way of illustrating a syntactical feature, vocabulary item, or aspect of Roman life, as a lighter and often amusing counterpoint to sober explanations of grammar and the edifying or stirring prose of a Cicero or a Seneca. The very form of epigram encourages reading Martial this way: these are brief poems that invite being detached from their context and read and enjoyed on their own. But of course they are, precisely, *poems*, and the literary qualities of Martial's work, perceptible only when one has read more than a few scattered pieces, were long underappreciated: its stimulating variety in subject matter and tone, its witty self-awareness, its careful construction. And two aspects of its subject matter in particular—frank humor about sex and elaborate flattery of the powerful—so offended the sensibilities of generations of scholars and teachers that they subjected Martial's work to stringent censorship, lest young minds be corrupted and older ones scandalized. Or so the argument went; Martial himself offers a few cogent responses (cf. 1.35, 7.10, 10.4, 11.15, and see Introduction, p. xxii).

Broad cultural changes over the past several decades, and with them a more open-minded and less judgmental approach to the study of Latin literature in all its variety, have put all that behind us. The 1991 publication of J. P. Sullivan's *Martial: The Unexpected Classic* ushered in a period of intense interest in this poet, of which one small but telling sign is the recent explosion in the genre of the scholarly commentary. When I was in graduate school only two of Martial's fifteen books of epigrams had a commentary; now only two do not, and that gap will no doubt soon be closed. Meanwhile, book-length studies (for example, those by William Fitzgerald and Victoria

Rimell) and a growing body of journal articles have begun to show what can happen when we read Martial's epigrams not just singly, or as evidence for social history, but as a poetic oeuvre. It is my hope that this edition will give students a taste of what makes Martial's poetry, Latin literature, and Roman culture so surprisingly vibrant that some of us keep coming back to it; and that, by engaging students in the sometimes challenging but always rewarding processes of reading Latin poetry, it will arouse in some a desire to learn more.

I am grateful to Ronnie Ancona for having invited me to undertake this project and for her reliably helpful presence throughout the process; to Laurie Haight Keenan of Bolchazy-Carducci for all her careful work; to the anonymous referees; and to the students in seminars on Martial and the Latin epigram that I have taught both in New York and in Berlin. This edition also owes a great deal to a year spent at the Freie Universität Berlin immersed in the study of Martial's poetry and to my commentary on Book 2 that came out of it; it is a pleasure to acknowledge the Ethyle Wolfe Institute for the Humanities at Brooklyn College and the Alexander von Humboldt Foundation for their generous research grants.

CRAIG WILLIAMS
New York

Introduction

❧ MARTIAL'S LIFE: BILBILIS AND ROME

Marcus Valerius Martialis was born between 38 and 41 CE in the Spanish hilltop town of Bilbilis, near modern Calatayud, about 60 km southwest of Zaragoza, in what was then the Roman province of Hispania Tarraconensis and today Aragón. He was evidently the son of Roman citizens named Valerius Fronto and Flaccilla and was born in the month of March, a fact that probably inspired his parents to give him the cognomen *Martialis*, traditionally anglicized as "Martial." The poet in one epigram (10.65) identifies himself with the mixed Celtic and Iberian ethnicity that was prevalent in much of Spain; presumably some of his ancestors had been granted the Roman citizenship at some point, perhaps when Bilbilis, an old Celtiberian settlement, was awarded the status of *municipium* by Augustus.

Martial moved to Rome in his mid-twenties in or around 64 CE, the year of the catastrophic fire that was rumored to have been started at the emperor Nero's orders, and one year before the Pisonian conspiracy in whose aftermath Seneca and Lucan among others were forced to commit suicide. Martial remained in Rome for about thirty-five years, apparently without interruption, except for one year spent in the town of Forum Cornelii (today Imola) in northern Italy, where he composed Book 3 of his epigrams around 87 CE; and at some point he acquired a country estate near Nomentum (today Mentana), about 25 km northeast of Rome. Martial thus lived in the city under a succession of emperors, from Nero through the Flavians (Vespasian and his sons Titus and Domitian) and finally Nerva. In 98 CE, the year of Nerva's death and Trajan's accession, Martial returned to Bilbilis. The reasons for his decision to leave Rome were no doubt complex: his poetry alludes to an increasing frustration with city life, but modern scholars have wondered about the timing of his move, only two years after the assassination of the emperor Domitian, regularly flattered by Martial in life but hated by many and much criticized after his death. In any case, Martial published another book of epigrams from Bilbilis in 101 CE (this may or may not be completely identical to the current Book 12), and in or about 104 CE Pliny the Younger wrote a letter (*Epistulae* 3.21) in which he reports with regret the news of Martial's recent death in Spain. The poet thus lived to his mid-sixties.

Rather than pursuing the traditional paths for financial and social success—politics, the military, or oratory, whether as a teacher in the schools or as a courtroom lawyer—Martial devoted himself to the writing and publication of poetry. While he may have lived partially off an inheritance or family resources, Roman poets of his day openly relied on the support of wealthy patrons: if there are enough Mae-cenases, Martial pointedly observes in one epigram, Vergils won't be lacking (8.55). And so he sought and obtained the support of a number of well-placed men, many of whom are also mentioned by his contemporary Statius: these patrons included men such as Decianus, Regulus, Atedius Melior, and L. Arruntius Stella; and women such as the widow of the poet Lucan. Despite Martial's periodic complaints of poverty, it is clear that he was never in desperate straits, and indeed seems to have had a comfortable lifestyle. In Book 1 he writes of a third-floor apartment on the Quirinal Hill,* but in later books he de-scribes a house in the city, and he never seems to have gone without slaves. At some point he attained the status of *eques,* which required assets of at least 400,000 sesterces. At some point, too, he acquired the estate near Nomentum: it has been speculated that this was a gift from one of his patrons, but we cannot know.

---

* For an online map of imperial Rome from William R. Shepherd's *Historical Atlas* (New York: Henry Holt and Company, 1929), go to http://tinyurl.com/26cm9h3 (http://upload.wikimedia.org/wikipedia/commons/e/e7/Shepherd-c-022-023.jpg).

Nor do we know whether Martial ever married or had any children. Pliny makes no mention of widow or heirs, but this may or may not have significance. At the end of Book 2, Martial prominently advertises the fact that the emperor has granted him the *ius trium liberorum*, a set of legal privileges (including the capacity to receive bequests from friends and patrons) normally reserved for men who had fathered three children, and Martial underscores that in doing so, the emperor is granting him something that Fortune has hitherto denied (2.91.5: *quod fortuna vetat fieri permitte videri*). This has been taken to imply that he was married but childless, but it might also mean that he was married but had fewer than three children, or just possibly that Fortune had willed that he never marry at all. In any case, we cannot draw any conclusions from his poetry itself, since the voice he adopts in the epigrams (see below) is sometimes that of a married man, sometimes that of an apparently confirmed bachelor. But one thing is clear: the fact that he received this privilege hints at the effectiveness of the connections he had made and the success his poetry had brought him in Rome.

ᕝ *Publication*

Martial's surviving oeuvre consists of fifteen books containing a total of over 1,500 poems, published over the span of more than two decades, from about 80 to about 101 CE. The term "publication" may be misleading, however, at least in the modern sense: Martial's epigrams became publicly available and reached audiences in a variety of contexts and on a range of scales. Individual epigrams might be recited, singly or in various combinations, by the poet or others at dinner parties as well as other private or public settings. In written form, small collections (some of them perhaps dedicated to one or another of Martial's patrons, but the hypothesis is controversial) circulated more or less privately: these may have gone by the name *libelli,* a term that can refer to a variety of written documents. Larger collections, corresponding to the books we now have or various combinations of them, were available for purchase at booksellers, some of whose names and locations Martial advertises. In that form, his poetry reached a broad audience indeed, both in Rome and throughout the empire: Martial boasts of readers even in far-off Britain.

Martial may have begun writing and circulating epigrams soon after his arrival in Rome in the mid-60s CE or even earlier in Bilbilis, but the earliest of the extant collections, which bears the generic title *Epigrammaton liber* in the manuscripts but is usually referred to as the *Liber spectaculorum* or *Liber de spectaculis*, celebrates the dedication of the Flavian Amphitheater—now more commonly known as the Colosseum—in 80 CE and was presumably published in that year or very shortly thereafter (it has occasionally been argued that the collection was published to mark not the dedication of the Colosseum under Titus but a somewhat later event under Domitian). Four or five years later came the publication of two books of couplets written to accompany items of food, drink, and other gifts given at the Saturnalia: Martial seems to have entitled them *Xenia* and *Apophoreta* respectively, but later (presumably after the poet's death) they were included at the end of his collected works and identified as Books 13 and 14, even though the numbers do not correspond to their chronological sequence. Beginning in about 86 CE Martial then published collections of epigrams on varied topics at approximately one-year intervals, identifying them with the numbers they still bear: Books 1–12.

As Ovid had done with the *Amores,* Martial also published revised editions of some of his poetry. Book 10, for example, originally came out in 95 CE, while the emperor Domitian was still alive, and was followed about a year later by Book 11, published in December 96, a few months after Domitian's assassination and the accession of Nerva. Two years later, however, Martial brought out a revised edition of Book 10, which is the version we now have; moreover, an epigram in Book 12, published several years after that, refers to an abridged edition of Books 10 and 11 together (12.4). It has also been hypothesized that around 93 CE Martial published a revised edition of Books 1–7; this may or may not have coincided with the publication of an edition in the relatively unusual codex format that Martial advertises at the beginning of Book 1.

ꙮ *Epigram before and after Martial*

Unlike many other Roman poets—including his contemporary Statius, from whom we have thirty-two poems on various topics, called *Silvae*, as well as two epics: the *Thebaid* and the unfinished *Achilleid*—Martial published in just one genre. A letter of Pliny's (*Epistulae* 4.14) shows that a number of labels could be given to poems of this type: *poematia, eclogae, idyllia, hendecasyllabi*. The term Martial himself favors is *epigrammata*, a Greek word that points to the historical origins of the genre: text written on (*epi-graphein*) objects ranging from cult statues to funerary monuments. Even as this type of poetry took on a life of its own and the poems were no longer attached to objects, epigrams always displayed salient characteristics of inscriptions. Above all, they tended to be brief and memorable and to be anchored in concrete situations, describing and commenting on specific objects or events; and the characteristic meter of inscriptional poetry, the elegiac couplet, was by far the most common meter of epigram as a literary form.

Martial was writing in a genre that flourished in both Greek and Latin. Greek epigrams by a variety of poets were gathered in anthologies or "garlands," including one by Meleager, probably around 100 BCE, and another by Philip in the first century CE. These were subsequently excerpted and supplemented with epigrams from other anthologies to form the large extant collection known as the *Palatine Anthology*, datable to the tenth century CE and containing about 3,700 epigrams organized in fifteen books. Among the poets represented in this anthology, those who predate Martial include Asclepiades, Callimachus, Posidippus, and Lucillius, who seems to have been especially influential on him. Recurring themes are the commemoration of the dead, the elaborate description of works of art, the portrayal (sometimes bemused, sometimes critical) of amusing or odd human behavior, and symposiastic and erotic topics like the pleasures of drinking, the beauty of youth, or the ephemerality of love. Among the Latin epigrammatists whom Martial cites as his predecessors are Albinovanus Pedo, Cornelius Lentulus Gaetulicus, Domitius Marsus, and above all Catullus, whose influence on Martial is extensive. Catullus' poetry illustrates certain traits that are especially characteristic of Latin epigram: a strong inclination (shared with that quintessentially Roman genre, *satura*) toward making social commentary by means of humor, invective, or a combination of both; a panoply of memorable characters; a propensity for blunt descriptions of sexual situations and bodily functions, not infrequently using obscene language.

This, then, was the tradition within which Martial composed his poetry, and to which he made an immense contribution. For he has long been recognized as a master of the genre, not only because of the sheer volume of his production but also because of the richness and variety of his subject matter and language, his clever wit and keen observation, his memorable phrasing, his ability to quickly create a scenario and deliver incisive commentary—often in a sharp point at the epigram's end, sometimes its final word, sometimes all of this in a single couplet. His influence is perceptible in all subsequent Latin epigrammatic poetry, including the work of the fourth-century CE poet Ausonius and the epigrams collected in what is now called the *Anthologia Latina,* and he remained an important model for all who subsequently composed in the genre in European languages. A much-quoted poem by Samuel Taylor Coleridge (1772–1834) shows Martial's influence in its self-referentiality, concision, and point, its carefully balanced structure, and its emphasis on cleverness and wit:

> *What is an epigram? A dwarfish whole,*
> *Its body brevity, and wit its soul.*

❧ *Themes*

Martial periodically reminds his readers of what sets his poetry apart: its nearness to everyday life. Epigram explicitly distinguishes itself from weightier and more serious genres treating grand mythological themes—epic and tragedy above all—precisely in its insistent focus on life in the contemporary city and on the panorama of behavior on display there: the everyday, the laughable, the scandalous. "My page," Martial proclaims, "has a human flavor" (*hominem pagina nostra sapit,* 10.5.10), and he writes about a wide range of characters indeed—men and women, Roman and foreign, rich and poor, free and slave, emperors and prostitutes—in a variety of urban settings: bathhouses and private dinner parties, porticoes and amphitheaters, public latrines and brothels.

This poetry gives us fascinating glimpses into the social landscape of late first-century CE Rome as perceived by a male member of the comfortable upper classes. We read of money-lending (2.3, 2.44) and legacy-hunting (1.10, 2.26, 4.56, 6.63, 10.8) as well as a range of bad behavior in connection with dining: hosts saving the best food and wine for themselves (1.20), guests stealing food to take home (2.37) or failing to reciprocate the favor of an invitation (3.27). More generally, we read of people failing to live up to the ideal of exchange on which a whole set of interpersonal relationships rested, especially patronage and friendship, and conjugal relations are a frequent target too: Martial writes of husbands who jokingly (?) wish they could get rid of their wives (4.24) and of wives who kill their husbands (9.15). There are jokes about doctors (1.47), about men who dye their hair (3.43) or depilate themselves (2.62), about women who buy false teeth (1.72). Gossip about others' sexual lives (1.24, 1.34, 2.28, 7.10) shares the pages with lofty celebrations of brotherly love (1.36), friendship (1.93), and a master's passion for his beautiful slave (11.26), along with elegant flattery of the powerful, especially the emperor (spect. 1–2, 1.14, 5.5). We read of men who immortalize their lapdogs in painted portraits (1.109) and of parrots who say "Hail Caesar" (14.73). Through all of this, Martial's tone ranges from the neutrally descriptive to the witty and playful: he sometimes criticizes and even condemns, but never with the bitter indignation or vitriol for which Juvenal's satires are renowned.

ᖇ *Characters and names*

Although Martial sometimes populates this varied urban landscape with anonymous men and women ("look at that man who . . ."), he frequently names names. Some of these are real, and in some cases external evidence gives us more knowledge: this is true of people like Arruntius Stella, Arria, Quintilian, Earinos, and of course the various emperors. Often, however, Martial's epigrams are our only source of knowledge about the individuals they name (Julius Martialis, for example, or Marcella of Bilbilis). It is important to keep in mind that relatively few readers from Martial's day to ours have known much, if anything at all, about the men and women named in his poetry—about who, say, Decianus is. Without the aid of a commentary, most readers of an epigram will only know what the poem itself says or suggests about the individuals it names, yet that is almost always enough to allow a rewarding reading. Regardless of how much we know about the people to whom they refer, the prominent presence of proper names in Martial's poetry has at least two important effects. Within a given epigram they create a lively, conversational atmosphere, and the accumulation of names over the course of Martial's oeuvre locates him in an extensive social network, advertising his connections to a variety of acquaintances, friends, and patrons all the way up to the emperor himself.

In the preface to Book 1 Martial makes a programmatic statement to the effect that, unlike such earlier poets as Catullus (who published some harsh words on none less than Julius Caesar), he will refrain from attacking people by their real names, and in Book 10 he summarizes the principle his poetry follows with a memorable phrase: *parcere personis, dicere de vitiis* (10.33.10). Thus we can be confident that names like Postumus, Zoilus, Galla, and the many others who are ridiculed or exposed in Martial's poetry are fictional. What we cannot know is whether any or all of them are pseudonyms for real people whom Martial knew, or are instead fictional *characters* whom he created on the basis of a range of behaviors and personalities familiar to him and his contemporary readers. Further complicating matters is that, while some of the pseudonyms clearly designate a variety of different characters rather than a single, coherent figure, others refer to one and the same character in a range of poems within a given book—and in a few instances, it seems, even across books whose publication was separated by a number of years. This raises an important question about reading practices. If a man called "Caecilianus" is described in a certain way in an epigram published in Book 2, how relevant is this to an epigram using the same name but published in, say, Book 10, at least eight years later? A few particularly attentive readers—especially those equipped with the modern tools of a concordance, index, or searchable database—may read such epigrams together and find some meaningful connections. Most readers over the centuries, however, have not made the effort or even paid much attention to the recurrence of the names, but have nonetheless arrived at rewarding readings of the epigrams—which, as we will see below, invite being read both as parts of a whole and as independent compositions.

ᴓ *Poet and reader*

Arguably the most prominent character in Martial's poetry is Martial himself, or rather the persona he adopts as the speaker or narrator. Here, too, the situation is more complex than one might at first think. To be sure, the stance is often straightforwardly autobiographical, i.e., the "I" who speaks corresponds to the real man M. Valerius Martialis: I come from Bilbilis, I am now living in Rome, I have written several books of epigrams, I am on friendly terms with men like Stertinius Avitus or Arruntius Stella. Yet in a few epigrams the speaker just as clearly cannot be identified with M. Valerius Martialis in any simple way: for example, the "I" who speaks in an epigram included in a book published when Martial was in his fifties is a young man just growing his beard and rather loudly asserting his newly achieved adult status (11.39). In most epigrams, in fact, the relationship of the first-person speaker to the historical figure M. Valerius Martialis is not easy to pin down: is the "I" fully autobiographical, completely fictional, or something in between? In short, the speaker in Martial's oeuvre invites being interpreted as a character whose circumstances, attitudes, and beliefs are largely but not entirely consistent and only partially coextensive with those of the man who wrote these poems.

That is one way to explain some significant internal contradictions. Sometimes, for example, Martial writes in the voice of the unmarried man and confirmed bachelor, sometimes—even within the same book—as an experienced husband: compare 11.19 and 11.104.

He almost always writes in the voice of a relatively poor poet who has no interest in a remunerative career in oratory (cf. 2.30), yet in one epigram he represents himself as having engaged to defend a man in court for 2,000 sesterces (8.17). We sometimes find contradictory *attitudes* as well. Often critical of those who hunt for a place in someone's will (especially by courting rich but repugnant old women) and of those who go to great lengths to obtain invitations to dinner, Martial sometimes speaks in the voice of a man who does precisely those things (cf. 10.8). At times he criticizes others for their abuse of their slaves, especially for trivial reasons (cf. 2.66: Lalage has beaten her hairdresser because of a misplaced hairpin), but the speaker in 8.23 has not only beaten his cook for ruining a meal but adds a question that may or may not be ironic: If you can't beat your cook for something like that, what can you beat him for?

To some extent, then, the epigrams invite being read as exercises in creating a character and speaking in that voice, as acts of poetic ventriloquism, as a further illustration of that variety that is so important to this poetry's self-image. Yet there are clearly limitations. After all, despite Roman writers' periodic insistence on the distinction between poet and poetry (cf. 11.15 along with Catullus 16), there was and still is a strong tradition of drawing conclusions about poets precisely from the nature of their poetry. Typical is Cicero's assertion that the archaic Greek poet Ibycus was highly susceptible to erotic passion—a conclusion Cicero draws solely from Ibycus' writings (Cicero *Tusc.* 4.71: *maxime vero omnium flagrasse amore Reginum Ibycum apparet ex scriptis*). It is not coincidental that in his poetry Martial never adopts a perspective or plays a role that would be seriously shaming or otherwise risky for him as a Roman man living in his social circles. The first-person speaker is always a man, and a comfortably gendered one at that: he never places himself in the role of effeminate womanizer, *cunnilingus*, *fellator*, or *cinaedus*, and he consistently distances himself from those roles by the time-honored techniques of bemused commentary or open ridicule. Nor does Martial ever write in the persona of a man belonging to a distinctly lower social class, for example the urban poor or slaves; nor does he ever openly criticize a living emperor.

Along with the poet, another key character in Martial's poetry is the reader, who appears sometimes as part of a collective plural (*vos*), sometimes as a singular but anonymous *lector*. Martial directly addresses his readers with a frequency unparalleled in Latin poetry before him and approximated only by Ovid, drawing them into what he hopes will be a mutually rewarding relationship: I can give you pleasure, you can give me lasting fame. Readers and reading are a prominent feature on the landscape of Martial's Rome—this is a world in which editions of authors like Cicero or Catullus, Vergil or Lucan were given as gifts at the Saturnalia (14.194–195, 14.203)—but the degree of attention Martial pays to his readers is unusually high, one of a number of ways in which this poetry shows an intense, even unrelenting self-consciousness. Anticipating modern interest in readerly processes and in the reception of texts, Martial uses some striking metaphors to describe the relations among poet, poetry, and readership (1.35, 10.2); tells his readers where they can buy a copy of his work (1.2); warns them of the variety in quality they will find when they read it (1.16); and worries that they may nonetheless become bored if they do (2.1).

∾ *Book structure*

Martial periodically emphasizes that we are reading epigram books *as such*, i.e., not random gatherings of poems. Whereas in the case of some earlier Latin poets, perhaps most notoriously Catullus, it is debatable whether the author himself or some later editor was responsible for the book in its current shape, we can be confident that Martial arranged the books as we have them now. Some show a tight unity in content or form: the *Liber spectaculorum* is dedicated to the new Flavian Amphitheater, and the *Xenia* (Book 13) and *Apophoreta* (Book 14) are collections of monodistichs (epigrams consisting of a single elegiac couplet) on items of food and drink and other gifts given at the Saturnalia. Books 5 and 8 have a thematic unity of another kind, advertising themselves as being entirely suitable for women and children and, unlike Martial's other books, forswearing lascivious language, whereas Book 11 associates itself with the Saturnalia and is especially lively, rambunctious, and at times obscene.

Otherwise, the individual books are characterized by a wide variety in subject, tone, and organization. Yet certain structural features recur. Every book opens, and most also close, with epigrams on one or both of two themes important to the oeuvre as a whole: the emperor, and Martial's poetry itself. Often there are significant juxtapositions and sequences, such that poems A and B form a thematic pair, and occasionally B explicitly responds to or openly comments on A. In another pattern, sets of epigrams on a specific character (such as Postumus, named in seven epigrams in Book 2) or theme (such as the hare and the lion, the subject of seven poems in Book 1) are not juxtaposed but scattered through a book. Epigrams belonging to such sets, sometimes called "cycles," invite being read *both* as independent compositions *and* as parts of a larger whole, and some readers have detected logical or thematic development within the cycles.

Book 3 provides an especially amusing illustration of how Martial's poetry can play with its self-awareness as a structured body of text. More than halfway through the book we come upon an epigram that warns the respectable married ladies among its readership that they should stop reading now—even as it ironically observes that this very warning will probably arouse their curiosity all the more (3.68). And so it is: the following epigrams are filled with frank descriptions of sexual practices and make liberal use of verbal obscenity. About twenty epigrams later, however, we encounter a poem (3.86) addressed to an anonymous female reader and culminating with a teasing remark indeed: Here you are, still reading me!

Martial's poetry, in short, invites being read in two different but not mutually exclusive ways: selectively, or straight through from beginning to end. An awareness of the possibilities and risks of *selective* reading periodically surfaces in Martial's poetry: we find a number of epigrams encouraging us to read only what we like but reminding us that we cannot expect to like everything we read. The *sequential* reading of an entire book is regrettably precluded by anthologies such as this one, but I have included a number of brief sequences of epigrams by way of giving a glimpse at the possibilities opened up by juxtaposition, continuity, and contrast. My hope is that readers of this edition will be inspired to try out an entire book of Martial's epigrams from beginning to end.

∾ *Poem structure and tips for reading*

Questions of structure are also important to a reading of individual epigrams themselves. By deliberately not providing introductory summaries of the epigrams it includes, this edition aims to give readers some experience in the characteristic challenge of reading Martial, and indeed any epigrammatic poetry. You pick a poem and simply begin reading, without any indication of what the topic is: the scenario and themes unfold more or less quickly as you read, and the point or joke emerges by the poem's end. The making of meaning from a brief poem is an important part of the pleasure of reading this genre, and perceiving structure is an important part of the process.

Nearly eighty percent of Martial's epigrams are composed in elegiac couplets, and these poems invite being read with attention to the individual couplet as basic structural unit: couplets are regularly, but not always, demarcated by syntax and sense. As you read an epigram in this meter, consider the internal structure of each couplet (hexameter followed by pentameter, the latter divided in two by the caesura). How are phrases, clauses, and sentences accommodated to the metrical framework? Does the pentameter expand upon or respond to the hexameter? Does each half of the pentameter consist of a self-contained unit of syntax or sense, or are the two halves intertwined, for example in a structure in which the final word of the first half modifies the final word of the second half? Then, as you move from one couplet to the next, observe the extent to which each is demarcated from the other by sense and/or syntax, and look for progressions in thought and language. Especially characteristic of Martial's poetry is the monodistich: how does a two-line poem manage so quickly to create a scenario and make a point? Finally, regardless of meter, structure, or length, Martial's epigrams are well known for their tendency to build up to a memorable, forceful, or unexpected final point. Pay particular attention to the final couplet or verse of each epigram. Does it revert to any words or images of the poem's opening line or couplet? Does it expand on what has preceded, does it represent a logical culmination or smoothly flowing conclusion, or is there some surprise?

Regardless of their meter or length, it has long been noted that many of Martial's epigrams have a bipartite structure: first a situation or scenario is laid out, and then comes some kind of response or commentary. The poet, critic, and philosopher Gotthold Ephraim Lessing (1729–1781) proposed the terms *Erwartung* (an expectation created) and *Aufschluss* (information or explanation that comes in response) as a way of describing the two halves of a bipartite epigram, and in the wake of Lessing's influential distinction various other terms have been proposed, including *exposition* and *conclusion*, *report* and *commentary*, *objective* and *subjective*. Whatever terminology we use, one of the pleasures in reading a bipartite epigram lies in perceiving its two halves, the relationship between them, and where the transition between them occurs. It is important to keep in mind, however, that by no means all of Martial's epigrams lend themselves to this kind of analysis: some have a tripartite structure, for example, while others consist of a single movement from beginning to end.

❧ *Language and meter*

Fluctuating among the loftily poetic, the rhetorically pointed, the straightforwardly descriptive, and the frankly obscene, Martial's language is as varied as its subject matter and tone, but consistently clear and vivid: after all, this poetry hopes never to bore its readers. Martial himself periodically draws our attention to certain qualities of his language. He reminds his readers that unrestrained language and a sometimes aggressive stance (*lascivia, licentia,* and *mala lingua*), as well as obscenity—i.e., the use of certain Latin words such as *mentula, cunnus, futuere, pedicare*, which were excluded from the grander literary genres or polite conversation—are all inalienable characteristics of the epigrammatic genre. More than once Martial points out that this kind of poetry is not for prudes, and he makes the occasional sly jab at those, both men and women, who feign shock but read him nonetheless, and read him with pleasure.

The pleasures of Martial's language will, I hope, unfold as you read through this small selection. The main challenges consist of the numerous proper names and allusions to cultural practices and items of everyday life that would have been immediately familiar to Martial's contemporaries but not to today's readers. Moreover, a taste for clever turns of phrase and rhetorical effect, widespread among Latin authors of Martial's day, along with a noticeable striving for impact through concision, especially in the final verse, phrase, or even word, not infrequently results in compressed formulations that need to be deciphered or unpacked. Helping readers through these and similar difficulties is one of the principal tasks I have set myself in writing this commentary.

Martial uses a small number of meters, which are easily mastered and will be familiar to those who have read poets like Catullus or Ovid. The great majority of the 1,560 poems and 9,592 lines of Martial's oeuvre are in elegiac couplets: 79.10% of the poems, representing 68.98% of all verses. Nearly all of the rest are composed in one of two meters: hendecasyllables (15.25% of poems, representing 21.58% of total verses) and scazons, also known as choliambics (7.69% of poems, representing 8.17% of total verses). The tiny remainder (only 0.77% of Martial's poems and 1.25% of the total verses) is made up of seven epigrams (a total of seventy-three lines) in various iambic meters, four epigrams (a total of forty-six lines) in dactylic hexameters, and one two-line epigram in an iambic form known as the sotadean. The basic schemes of the three most common meters in Martial are given below; for more detailed discussion of these and all other meters of Latin poetry, the reader is referred to D. S. Raven's *Latin Metre*.

N.B. In the commentary I only indicate the meter of an epigram when it is *not* composed in elegiac couplets, which can be considered the default option in Martial.

Elegiac couplet

An elegiac couplet pairs a dactylic hexameter of the kind familiar from Vergil and Ovid with a so-called "pentameter" consisting of two dactylic half-verses (hemistichs) separated by a word break (caesura). The underlying scheme is thus as follows:

$$-\cup\cup\; / \; -\cup\cup\; / \; - \; \| \; \cup\cup\; / \; -\cup\cup\; / \; -\cup\cup\; / \; -\times$$
$$-\cup\cup\; / \; -\cup\cup\; / \; - \; \| \; -\cup\cup\; / \; -\cup\cup\; / \; -$$

If we consider a dactylic hexameter as consisting of the two halves, A and B, separated by a caesura after the first syllable of the third foot (the most common type of caesura, called "masculine" or "penthemimeral"), the elegiac couplet can thus be described as having the pattern ABAA.

The pure scheme given above almost never occurs, however, since any sequence of two short syllables can be substituted by a single long syllable: thus any foot except the last may take the form either of a dactyl (–∪∪) or of a spondee (– –). In the *hexameter*, however, this almost never happens in the fifth foot, so that the line almost always ends with the characteristic rhythm –∪∪ / –×. In the *pentameter*, the substitution of a long syllable for two shorts can occur *only in the first half of the line*, never in the second. The following scheme thus represents the shape of the overwhelming majority of elegiac couplets in Martial, the only variations consisting in the location of the caesura in the hexameter and the rare spondaic fifth foot in that line.

–∪∪ / –∪∪ / – || ∪∪ / –∪∪ / –∪∪ / –×
–∪∪ / –∪∪ / – || –∪∪ / –∪∪ / –

  – – / – – / – || – / – ∪ ∪ / – ∪ ∪ / – –
Ar-gi-/le-ta-/nas || *ma-/vis ha-bi-/ta-re ta-/ber-nas*

  – ∪ ∪ / – ∪ ∪ / – || – ∪ ∪ / – ∪ ∪ / –
  cum ti-bi, / par-ve li-/ber, || *scri-ni-a / nos-tra va-/cent*
(1.3.1–2)

  – ∪ ∪ / – ∪ ∪ / – || ∪ ∪ /–   – / – ∪ ∪/ – –
Mu-ne-ra / quod se-ni-/bus || *vi-du-/is-qu(e) in-/gen-ti-a / mit-tis,*

  – – / – ∪ ∪/ – || – ∪ ∪/– ∪ ∪ / –
  vis te / mu-ni-fi-/cum, || *Gar-gi-li-/a-ne, vo-/cem?*
(4.56.1–2)

One characteristic that sets Martial's elegiac couplets apart from those of the Augustan poets, and especially Ovid, is that whereas the earlier poets almost unvaryingly end the pentameter with disyllabic words only (exceptions are extremely rare and almost always proper names), Martial not infrequently has three-, four-, or even five-syllable words at the end of the couplet (e.g., *lacrimae* at 1.33.2 or *supercilium* at 1.24.2).

N.B. This edition follows the standard practice of indenting the pentameter by way of visually marking each couplet.

Phalaecian hendecasyllable

Whereas his predecessor Catullus allowed a number of variations, in Martial this stichic or line-by-line meter always takes the same form: two long syllables at the beginning are followed by a choriambic nucleus ($-\cup\cup-$) and a concluding element with the loosely iambic rhythm $\cup-\cup--$. The scheme is thus as follows:

$$- \; - \; / \; - \; \cup \; \cup \; - \; / \; \cup \; - \; \cup \; - \; -$$
vi-tam / quae fa-ci-ant / be-a-ti-o-rem
(10.47.1)

$$- \; - \; / \quad - \; \cup \; \cup \; - \; / \; \cup \; - \; \cup \; - \; -$$
o gran-/d(e) in-ge-ni-um / me-i so-da-lis
(2.44.10)

Scazon

The scazon, also known as the choliambus ("limping iamb"), is an iambic trimeter whose final iambic element ($\cup-$) is replaced by two longs ($--$), thus bringing the line to a dragged or "limping" close, culminating with three long syllables in a row. The underlying scheme is as follows:

$$\times \; - \; \cup \; - \; / \; \times \; - \; \cup \; - \; / \; \cup \; - \; - \; -$$

$$\cup \; - \; \cup \; - \; / \; - \; - \; \cup \; - \; / \; \cup \; - \; - \; -$$
pe-tit Ge-mel-/lus nup-ti-as / Ma-ro-nil-lae
(1.10.1)

Note that the effect at the end of the line is accentuated by the fact that the final iambic metron, unlike the first two, *always* begins with a short syllable. Furthermore, as usual with iambic meters, any long syllable may be resolved into two shorts, but in Martial's scazons this occurs much less rarely than, for example, in Plautus' iambic meters, and only in the first two metra. In any case, the line always ends with the characteristic rhythm ∪–––.

– ∪̑ ∪ ∪ – / ∪ –   ∪ – / ∪ – – –
et cu-pit et in-/stat et pre-ca-/tur et do-nat
(1.10.2)

∽ *Note on the text*

Manuscripts containing Martial's epigrams can be divided into three families, which are usually identified by the Greek letters α, β, and γ. Family α consists of three manuscripts dating to the ninth and tenth centuries, family β is represented by one twelfth-century manuscript and three from the fourteenth, and family γ includes (among others) four manuscripts from the tenth to the eleventh centuries. The division into three families can be traced back to late antiquity: manuscripts of family β descend from an edition of Martial's work done in 401 CE by a certain Torquatus Gennadius.

In general, Martial's text is in good shape. There are very few cruces (passages in which the manuscripts give a nonsensical or otherwise clearly incorrect reading but for which modern editors have been unable to come up with persuasive solutions) and relatively few passages in which the manuscripts offer more than one plausible reading: for an example in this anthology, see 2.5.3. It has been hypothesized that some of the latter might stem from revised editions published in Martial's lifetime; but some or all of them might also derive from unconscious or well-meaning corrections or outright errors made by later copyists.

Except at 2.30.3, 5.58.6, 7.14.9, and 12.3.7–12 (see commentary ad loc.), the text printed in this anthology is that of Lindsay's 1929 Oxford Classical Texts edition, with minor variations in punctuation and orthography.

∾ *Suggested reading*

Anderson, W. S. "*Lascivia* vs. *ira*. Martial and Juvenal." In *Essays on Roman Satire* (Princeton 1982), pp. 362–395.

Fagan, Garrett G. *Bathing in Public in the Roman World.* Ann Arbor 1999.

Fitzgerald, William. *Slavery and the Roman Literary Imagination.* New York and Cambridge 2000.

———. *Martial: The World of the Epigram.* Chicago and London 2007.

Fowler, Don P. "Martial and the Book." *Ramus* 24 (1995): 31–58.

Gowers, Emily. *The Loaded Table. Representations of Food in Roman Literature.* Oxford 1993.

Hinds, Stephen. *Allusion and Intertext. Dynamics of Appropriation in Roman Poetry.* Cambridge 1998.

———. "Martial's Ovid / Ovid's Martial." *Journal of Roman Studies* 97 (2007): 113–154.

Howell, Peter. *Martial.* London 2009.

Hutchinson, G. O. *Latin Literature from Seneca to Juvenal. A Critical Study.* Oxford 1993.

Nauta, Ruurd. *Poetry for Patrons. Literary Communication in the Age of Domitian.* Leiden 2002.

———, et al., eds. *Flavian Poetry.* Leiden 2005.

Nisbet, Gideon. *Greek Epigram in the Roman Empire: Martial's Forgotten Rivals.* Oxford and New York 2003.

Raven, D. S. *Latin Metre.* London 1965.

Rimell, Victoria. *Martial's Rome: Empire and the Ideology of Epigram.* Cambridge 2008.

Roman, Luke. "The Representation of Literary Materiality in Martial's Epigrams." *Journal of Roman Studies* 91 (2001): 113–145.

Saller, Richard. "Martial on Patronage and Literature." *Classical Quarterly* 33 (1983): 246–257.

Spisak, Art L. *Martial: A Social Guide.* London 2007.

Sullivan, J. P. *Martial: The Unexpected Classic*. Cambridge 1991.

Toynbee, J. M. C. *Animals in Roman Life and Art*. London 1973.

White, Peter. "*Amicitia* and the Profession of Poetry in Early Imperial Rome." *Journal of Roman Studies* 68 (1978): 74–92.

Williams, Craig. "Ovid, Martial, and Poetic Immortality. Traces of *Amores* 1.15 in the *Epigrams*." *Arethusa* 35 (2002): 417–433.

———. "*Sit nequior omnibus libellis*. Text, Poet, and Reader in Martial's Epigrams." *Philologus* 146 (2002): 150–171.

———. *Roman Homosexuality*. Second edition. Oxford and New York 2010.

———. *Reading Roman Friendship*. Cambridge (forthcoming).

Commentaries in English

Coleman, Kathleen. *M. Valerii Martialis Liber spectaculorum*. Oxford and New York 2006.

Galán Vioque, Guillermo. *Martial, Book VII: A Commentary*. Translated by J. J. Zoltowski. Leiden 2002.

Henriksén, Christer. *Martial, Book IX: A Commentary*. Uppsala 1999.

Howell, Peter. *A Commentary on Book One of the Epigrams of Martial*. London 1980.

———. *Martial: The Epigrams, Book 5*. Warminster 1995.

Kay, N. M. *Martial Book XI: A Commentary*. London 1985.

Leary, Timothy J. *Martial, Book XIV: The Apophoreta*. London 1996.

———. *Martial, Book XIII: The Xenia*. London 2001.

Moreno Soldevilla, Rosario. *Martial, Book IV: A Commentary*. Leiden 2006.

Watson, Lindsay, and Patricia Watson. *Martial: Select Epigrams*. Cambridge 2003.

Williams, Craig. *Martial, Epigrams: Book Two*. Oxford and New York 2004.

Latin Text

◈ *Liber spectaculorum*
spect. 1

 Barbara pyramidum sileat miracula Memphis,
  Assyrius iactet nec Babylona labor,
 nec Triviae templo molles laudentur Iones,
  dissimulet Delon cornibus ara frequens,
5 aëre nec vacuo pendentia Mausolea
  laudibus immodicis Cares in astra ferant.
 omnis Caesareo cedit labor Amphitheatro:
  unum pro cunctis fama loquetur opus.

spect. 2

 Hic ubi sidereus propius videt astra colossus
  et crescunt media pegmata celsa via,
 invidiosa feri radiabant atria regis
  unaque iam tota stabat in urbe domus.
5 hic ubi conspicui venerabilis Amphitheatri
  erigitur moles, stagna Neronis erant.
 hic ubi miramur velocia munera thermas,
  abstulerat miseris tecta superbus ager.
 Claudia diffusas ubi porticus explicat umbras,

1

10   ultima pars aulae deficientis erat.

    reddita Roma sibi est et sunt te praeside, Caesar,

       deliciae populi, quae fuerant domini.

spect. 7

    Qualiter in Scythica religatus rupe Prometheus

       adsiduam nimio pectore pavit avem,

    nuda Caledonio sic viscera praebuit urso

       non falsa pendens in cruce Laureolus.

5   vivebant laceri membris stillantibus artus

       inque omni nusquam corpore corpus erat.

    denique supplicium <* * *>

       vel domini iugulum foderat ense nocens,

    templa vel arcano demens spoliaverat auro,

10   subdiderat saevas vel tibi, Roma, faces.

    vicerat antiquae sceleratus crimina famae,

       in quo, quae fuerat fabula, poena fuit.

❧ *Book 1*

1.1

    Hic est quem legis ille, quem requiris,

    toto notus in orbe Martialis

    argutis epigrammaton libellis:

    cui, lector studiose, quod dedisti

5   viventi decus atque sentienti,

    rari post cineres habent poetae.

1.2

Qui tecum cupis esse meos ubicumque libellos
    et comites longae quaeris habere viae,
hos eme, quos artat brevibus membrana tabellis:
    scrinia da magnis, me manus una capit.
5   ne tamen ignores ubi sim venalis et erres
    urbe vagus tota, me duce certus eris:
libertum docti Lucensis quaere Secundum
    limina post Pacis Palladiumque forum.

1.3

Argiletanas mavis habitare tabernas,
    cum tibi, parve liber, scrinia nostra vacent.
nescis, heu, nescis dominae fastidia Romae:
    crede mihi, nimium Martia turba sapit.
5   maiores nusquam rhonchi: iuvenesque senesque
    et pueri nasum rhinocerotis habent.
audieris cum grande "sophos," dum basia iactas,
    ibis ab excusso missus in astra sago.
sed tu ne totiens domini patiare lituras
10   neve notet lusus tristis harundo tuos,
aetherias, lascive, cupis volitare per auras.
    i, fuge; sed poteras tutior esse domi.

1.6

Aetherias aquila puerum portante per auras
    inlaesum timidis unguibus haesit onus;
nunc sua Caesareos exorat praeda leones
    tutus et ingenti ludit in ore lepus.
5   quae maiora putas miracula? summus utrisque
    auctor adest: haec sunt Caesaris, illa Iovis.

1.10

Petit Gemellus nuptias Maronillae
et cupit et instat et precatur et donat.
adeone pulchra est? immo foedius nil est.
quid ergo in illa petitur et placet? tussit.

1.13

Casta suo gladium cum traderet Arria Paeto,
    quem de visceribus strinxerat ipsa suis,
"si qua fides, vulnus quod feci non dolet," inquit,
    "sed tu quod facies, hoc mihi, Paete, dolet."

1.15

O mihi post nullos, Iuli, memorande sodales,
    si quid longa fides canaque iura valent:
bis iam paene tibi consul tricensimus instat,
    et numerat paucos vix tua vita dies.
5   non bene distuleris videas quae posse negari,
    et solum hoc ducas, quod fuit, esse tuum.

exspectant curaeque catenatique labores;

　　gaudia non remanent, sed fugitiva volant.

haec utraque manu complexuque adsere toto;

10　　saepe fluunt imo sic quoque lapsa sinu.

non est, crede mihi, sapientis dicere "vivam."

　　sera nimis vita est crastina. vive hodie!

1.16

Sunt bona, sunt quaedam mediocria, sunt mala plura

　　quae legis hic. aliter non fit, Avite, liber.

1.20

Dic mihi, quis furor est? turba spectante vocata

　　solus boletos, Caeciliane, voras.

quid dignum tanto tibi ventre gulaque precabor?

　　boletum qualem Claudius edit, edas.

1.24

Aspicis incomptis illum, Deciane, capillis,

　　cuius et ipse times triste supercilium,

qui loquitur Curios adsertoresque Camillos?

　　nolito fronti credere: nupsit heri.

1.32

Non amo te, Sabidi, nec possum dicere quare.

　　hoc tantum possum dicere: non amo te.

1.33

> Amissum non flet cum sola est Gellia patrem;
>   si quis adest, iussae prosiliunt lacrimae.
> non luget quisquis laudari, Gellia, quaerit;
>   ille dolet vere qui sine teste dolet.

1.34

> Incustoditis et apertis, Lesbia, semper
>   liminibus peccas, nec tua furta tegis,
> et plus spectator quam te delectat adulter,
>   nec sunt grata tibi gaudia si qua latent.
> 5 at meretrix abigit testem veloque seraque
>   raraque Submemmi fornice rima patet.
> a Chione saltem vel ab Iade disce pudorem:
>   abscondunt spurcas et monumenta lupas.
> numquid dura tibi nimium censura videtur?
> 10   deprendi veto te, Lesbia, non futui.

1.35

> Versus scribere me parum severos
> nec quos praelegat in schola magister,
> Corneli, quereris. sed hi libelli,
> tamquam coniugibus suis mariti,
> 5 non possunt sine mentula placere.
> quid si me iubeas thalassionem
> verbis dicere non thalassionis?

quis Floralia vestit et stolatum

permittit meretricibus pudorem?

10   lex haec carminibus data est iocosis,

ne possint, nisi pruriant, iuvare.

quare deposita severitate

parcas lusibus et iocis rogamus,

nec castrare velis meos libellos:

15   gallo turpius est nihil Priapo.

1.36

Si, Lucane, tibi vel si tibi, Tulle, darentur

    qualia Ledaei fata Lacones habent,

nobilis haec esset pietatis rixa duobus,

    quod pro fratre mori vellet uterque prior,

5   diceret infernas et qui prior isset ad umbras:

    "vive tuo, frater, tempore, vive meo."

1.37

Ventris onus misero—nec te pudet—excipis auro,

    Basse; bibis vitro. carius ergo cacas.

1.47

Nuper erat medicus, nunc est vispillo Diaulus.

    quod vispillo facit, fecerat et medicus.

1.72

Nostris versibus esse te poetam,
Fidentine, putas cupisque credi?
sic dentata sibi videtur Aegle
emptis ossibus Indicoque cornu;
5   sic, quae nigrior est cadente moro,
cerussata sibi placet Lycoris.
hac et tu ratione qua poeta es,
calvus cum fueris, eris comatus.

1.93

Fabricio iunctus fido requiescit Aquinus,
    qui prior Elysias gaudet adisse domos.
ara duplex primi testatur munera pili;
    plus tamen est, titulo quod breviore legis:
5   "iunctus uterque sacro laudatae foedere vitae,
    famaque quod raro novit, amicus erat."

1.109

Issa est passere nequior Catulli,
Issa est purior osculo columbae,
Issa est blandior omnibus puellis,
Issa est carior Indicis lapillis,
5   Issa est deliciae catella Publi.
hanc tu, si queritur, loqui putabis;
sentit tristitiamque gaudiumque.

collo nixa cubat capitque somnos,

ut suspiria nulla sentiantur,

10   et desiderio coacta ventris

gutta pallia non fefellit ulla,

sed blando pede suscitat toroque

deponi monet et rogat levari.

castae tantus inest pudor catellae,

15   ignorat Venerem; nec invenimus

dignum tam tenera virum puella.

hanc ne lux rapiat suprema totam,

picta Publius exprimit tabella,

in qua tam similem videbis Issam,

20   ut sit tam similis sibi nec ipsa.

Issam denique pone cum tabella:

aut utramque putabis esse veram,

aut utramque putabis esse pictam.

1.110

Scribere me quereris, Velox, epigrammata longa.

ipse nihil scribis: tu breviora facis.

1.118

Cui legisse satis non est epigrammata centum,

nil illi satis est, Caediciane, mali.

ᘰ *Book 2*

2.5

Ne valeam, si non totis, Deciane, diebus
    et tecum totis noctibus esse velim.
sed duo sunt quae nos disiungunt milia passum;
    quattuor haec fiunt, cum rediturus eam.
5   saepe domi non es; cum sis quoque, saepe negaris:
    vel tantum causis vel tibi saepe vacas.
te tamen ut videam, duo milia non piget ire;
    ut te non videam, quattuor ire piget.

2.11

Quod fronte Selium nubila vides, Rufe,
quod ambulator porticum terit seram,
lugubre quiddam quod tacet piger vultus,
quod paene terram nasus indecens tangit,
5   quod dextra pectus pulsat et comam vellit:
non ille amici fata luget aut fratris,
uterque natus vivit et precor vivat,
salva est et uxor sarcinaeque servique,
nihil colonus vilicusque decoxit.
10 maeroris igitur causa quae? domi cenat.

2.18

Capto tuam, pudet heu, sed capto, Maxime, cenam,
    tu captas aliam; iam sumus ergo pares.
mane salutatum venio, tu diceris isse
    ante salutatum; iam sumus ergo pares.

5   sum comes ipse tuus tumidique anteambulo regis,

       tu comes alterius; iam sumus ergo pares.

    esse sat est servum, iam nolo vicarius esse.

       qui rex est regem, Maxime, non habeat.

2.19

Felicem fieri credis me, Zoile, cena?

    felicem cena, Zoile, deinde tua?

debet Aricino conviva recumbere clivo,

    quem tua felicem, Zoile, cena facit.

2.20

Carmina Paulus emit, recitat sua carmina Paulus.

    nam quod emas possis iure vocare tuum.

2.21

Basia das aliis, aliis das, Postume, dextram.

    dicis "utrum mavis? elige." malo manum.

2.22

Quid mihi vobiscum est, o Phoebe novemque sorores?

    ecce nocet vati Musa iocosa suo.

dimidio nobis dare Postumus ante solebat

    basia, nunc labro coepit utroque dare.

2.23

Non dicam, licet usque me rogetis,
qui sit Postumus in meo libello,
non dicam. quid enim mihi necesse est
has offendere basiationes,
5   quae se tam bene vindicare possunt?

2.26

Quod querulum spirat, quod acerbum Naevia tussit,
    inque tuos mittit sputa subinde sinus,
iam te rem factam, Bithynice, credis habere?
    erras. blanditur Naevia, non moritur.

2.28

Rideto multum qui te, Sextille, cinaedum
    dixerit, et digitum porrigito medium.
sed nec pedico es nec tu, Sextille, fututor,
    calda Vetustinae nec tibi bucca placet.
5   ex istis nihil es, fateor, Sextille. quid ergo es?
    nescio, sed tu scis res superesse duas.

2.30

Mutua viginti sestertia forte rogabam,
    quae vel donanti non grave munus erat:
quippe rogabatur fidusque vetusque sodalis
    et cuius laxas arca flagellat opes.
5   is mihi "dives eris, si causas egeris" inquit.
    quod peto da, Gai: non peto consilium.

2.37

Quidquid ponitur hinc et inde verris,
mammas suminis imbricemque porci
communemque duobus attagenam,
mullum dimidium lupumque totum
5   muraenaeque latus femurque pulli
stillantemque alica sua palumbum.
haec cum condita sunt madente mappa,
traduntur puero domum ferenda;
nos accumbimus otiosa turba.
10   ullus si pudor est, repone cenam.
cras te, Caeciliane, non vocavi.

2.44

Emi seu puerum togamve pexam
seu tres, ut puta, quattuorve libras,
Sextus protinus ille fenerator
quem nostis, veterem meum sodalem,
5   ne quid forte petam timet cavetque
et secum, sed ut audiam, susurrat:
"septem milia debeo Secundo,
Phoebo quattuor, undecim Phileto,
et quadrans mihi nullus est in arca."
10   o grande ingenium mei sodalis!
durum est, Sexte, negare cum rogaris;
quanto durius, antequam rogeris.

2.62

> Quod pectus, quod crura tibi, quod bracchia vellis,
>> quod cincta est brevibus mentula tonsa pilis:
> hoc praestas, Labiene, tuae—quis nescit?—amicae.
>> cui praestas, culum quod, Labiene, pilas?

2.80

> Hostem cum fugeret, se Fannius ipse peremit.
>> hic, rogo, non furor est: ne moriare, mori?

2.82

> Abscisa servum quid figis, Pontice, lingua?
>> nescis tu populum, quod tacet ille, loqui?

ᴄ Book 3

3.1

> Hoc tibi, quidquid id est, longinquis mittit ab oris
>> Gallia Romanae nomine dicta togae.
> hunc legis et laudas librum fortasse priorem:
>> illa vel haec mea sunt, quae meliora putas.
> 5 plus sane placeat domina qui natus in urbe est:
>> debet enim Gallum vincere verna liber.

3.27

Numquam me revocas, venias cum saepe vocatus:
　　ignosco, nullum si modo, Galle, vocas.
invitas alios: vitium est utriusque. "quod?" inquis.
　　et mihi cor non est et tibi, Galle, pudor.

3.43

Mentiris iuvenem tinctis, Laetine, capillis,
　　tam subito corvus, qui modo cycnus eras.
non omnes fallis: scit te Proserpina canum.
　　personam capiti detrahet illa tuo.

∾ *Book 4*

4.24

Omnes quas habuit, Fabiane, Lycoris amicas
　　extulit. uxori fiat amica meae.

4.56

Munera quod senibus viduisque ingentia mittis,
　　vis te munificum, Gargiliane, vocem?
sordidius nihil est, nihil est te spurcius uno,
　　qui potes insidias dona vocare tuas.
5　sic avidis fallax indulget piscibus hamus,
　　callida sic stultas decipit esca feras.
quid sit largiri, quid sit donare docebo,
　　si nescis: dona, Gargiliane, mihi.

❧ *Book 5*

5.58

Cras te victurum, cras dicis, Postume, semper.

    dic mihi: cras istud, Postume, quando venit?

quam longe cras istud! ubi est? aut unde petendum?

    numquid apud Parthos Armeniosque latet?

5   iam cras istud habet Priami vel Nestoris annos.

    cras istud quanti, dic mihi, possit emi?

cras vives? hodie iam vivere, Postume, serum est.

    ille sapit quisquis, Postume, vixit heri.

5.81

Semper pauper eris, si pauper es, Aemiliane:

    dantur opes nullis nunc nisi divitibus.

5.83

Insequeris, fugio; fugis, insequor. haec mihi mens est:

    velle tuum nolo, Dindyme, nolle volo.

❧ *Book 6*

6.1

Sextus mittitur hic tibi libellus,

in primis mihi care Martialis;

quem si terseris aure diligenti,

audebit minus anxius tremensque

5   magnas Caesaris in manus venire.

6.34

Basia da nobis, Diadumene, pressa. "quot?" inquis.
　　Oceani fluctus me numerare iubes
et maris Aegaei sparsas per litora conchas
　　et quae Cecropio monte vagantur apes
5　quaeque sonant pleno vocesque manusque theatro,
　　cum populus subiti Caesaris ora videt.
nolo quot arguto dedit exorata Catullo
　　Lesbia; pauca cupit qui numerare potest.

∿ *Book 7*

7.5

Si desiderium, Caesar, populique patrumque
　　respicis et Latiae gaudia vera togae,
redde deum votis poscentibus. invidet hosti
　　Roma suo, veniat laurea multa licet:
5　terrarum dominum propius videt ille tuoque
　　terretur vultu barbarus et fruitur.

7.10

Pedicatur Eros, fellat Linus: Ole, quid ad te
　　de cute quid faciant ille vel ille sua?
centenis futuit Matho milibus: Ole, quid ad te?
　　non tu propterea, sed Matho pauper erit.
5　in lucem cenat Sertorius: Ole, quid ad te,
　　cum liceat tota stertere nocte tibi?

septingenta Tito debet Lupus: Ole, quid ad te?
    assem ne dederis crediderisve Lupo.
illud dissimulas ad te quod pertinet, Ole,
10   quodque magis curae convenit esse tuae.
pro togula debes: hoc ad te pertinet, Ole.
    quadrantem nemo iam tibi credit: et hoc.
uxor moecha tibi est: hoc ad te pertinet, Ole.
    poscit iam dotem filia grandis: et hoc.
15 dicere quindecies poteram quod pertinet ad te;
    sed quid agas ad me pertinet, Ole, nihil.

7.14

Accidit infandum nostrae scelus, Aule, puellae:
    amisit lusus deliciasque suas,
non quales teneri ploravit amica Catulli
    Lesbia, nequitiis passeris orba sui,
5   vel Stellae cantata meo quas flevit Ianthis,
    cuius in Elysio nigra columba volat.
lux mea non capitur nugis neque moribus istis
    nec dominae pectus talia damna movent.
bis senos puerum numerantem perdidit annos,
10   mentula cui nondum sesquipedalis erat.

∾ *Book 8*

8.12

Uxorem quare locupletem ducere nolim
    quaeritis? uxori nubere nolo meae.
inferior matrona suo sit, Prisce, marito.
    non aliter fiunt femina virque pares.

8.17

Egi, Sexte, tuam pactus duo milia causam;
    misisti nummos quod mihi mille, quid est?
"narrasti nihil" inquis "et a te perdita causa est."
    tanto plus debes, Sexte, quod erubui.

8.23

Esse tibi videor saevus nimiumque gulosus,
    qui propter cenam, Rustice, caedo cocum.
si levis ista tibi flagrorum causa videtur,
    ex qua vis causa vapulet ergo cocus?

8.55

Temporibus nostris aetas cum cedat avorum
    creverit et maior cum duce Roma suo,
ingenium sacri miraris desse Maronis
    nec quemquam tanta bella sonare tuba.
5   sint Maecenates, non derunt, Flacce, Marones;
    Vergiliumque tibi vel tua rura dabunt.

iugera perdiderat miserae vicina Cremonae,
    flebat et abductas Tityrus aeger oves;
risit Tuscus eques paupertatemque malignam
10   reppulit et celeri iussit abire fuga.
"accipe divitias et vatum maximus esto;
    tu licet et nostrum" dixit "Alexin ames."
adstabat domini mensis pulcherrimus ille
    marmorea fundens nigra Falerna manu,
15   et libata dabat roseis carchesia labris
    quae poterant ipsum sollicitare Iovem.
excidit attonito pinguis Galatea poetae
    Thestylis et rubras messibus usta genas;
protinus Italiam concepit et "Arma virumque,"
20   qui modo vix Culicem fleverat ore rudi.
quid Varios Marsosque loquar ditataque vatum
    nomina, magnus erit quos numerare labor?
ergo ero Vergilius, si munera Maecenatis
    des mihi? Vergilius non ero, Marsus ero.

❧ *Book 9*
9.praef.

Have, mi Torani, frater carissime. epigramma, quod extra
ordinem paginarum est, ad Stertinium clarissimum virum
scripsimus, qui imaginem meam ponere in bibliotheca sua
voluit. de quo scribendum tibi putavi, ne ignorares Avitus iste
quis vocaretur. vale et para hospitium.

Note, licet nolis, sublimi pectore vates,
    cui referet serus praemia digna cinis,
hoc tibi sub nostra breve carmen imagine vivat,
    quam non obscuris iungis, Avite, viris:
5   "Ille ego sum nulli nugarum laude secundus
    quem non miraris, sed—puto—, lector, amas.
maiores maiora sonent; mihi parva locuto
    sufficit in vestras saepe redire manus."

9.15

Inscripsit tumulis septem scelerata virorum
    "se fecisse" Chloe. quid pote simplicius?

9.70

Dixerat "O mores! O tempora!" Tullius olim,
    sacrilegum strueret cum Catilina nefas,
cum gener atque socer diris concurreret armis
    maestaque civili caede maderet humus.
5   cur nunc "O mores!" cur nunc "O tempora!" dicis?
    quod tibi non placeat, Caeciliane, quid est?
nulla ducum feritas, nulla est insania ferri;
    pace frui certa laetitiaque licet.
non nostri faciunt tibi quod tua tempora sordent,
10   sed faciunt mores, Caeciliane, tui.

↬ *Book 10*

10.4

    Qui legis Oedipoden caligantemque Thyesten,
        Colchidas et Scyllas, quid nisi monstra legis?
    quid tibi raptus Hylas, quid Parthenopaeus et Attis,
        quid tibi dormitor proderit Endymion,
5   exutusve puer pinnis labentibus? aut qui
        odit amatrices Hermaphroditus aquas?
    quid te vana iuvant miserae ludibria chartae?
        hoc lege, quod possit dicere vita: "meum est."
    non hic Centauros, non Gorgonas Harpyiasque
10   invenies; hominem pagina nostra sapit.
    sed non vis, Mamurra, tuos cognoscere mores
        nec te scire. legas Aetia Callimachi.

10.8

    Nubere Paula cupit nobis, ego ducere Paulam
        nolo: anus est. vellem, si magis esset anus.

10.47

    Vitam quae faciant beatiorem,
    iucundissime Martialis, haec sunt:
    res non parta labore sed relicta;
    non ingratus ager, focus perennis;
5   lis numquam, toga rara, mens quieta;
    vires ingenuae, salubre corpus;
    prudens simplicitas, pares amici;

convictus facilis, sine arte mensa;

nox non ebria sed soluta curis;

10   non tristis torus et tamen pudicus;

somnus qui faciat breves tenebras;

quod sis esse velis nihilque malis;

summum nec metuas diem nec optes.

∾ *Book 11*

11.13

Quisquis Flaminiam teris, viator,

noli nobile praeterire marmor.

urbis deliciae salesque Nili,

ars et gratia, lusus et voluptas,

5   Romani decus et dolor theatri

atque omnes Veneres Cupidinesque

hoc sunt condita, quo Paris, sepulchro.

11.14

Heredes, nolite brevem sepelire colonum:

nam terra est illi quantulacumque gravis.

11.15

Sunt chartae mihi quas Catonis uxor

et quas horribiles legant Sabinae;

hic totus volo rideat libellus

et sit nequior omnibus libellis.

5   qui vino madeat nec erubescat

　　pingui sordidus esse Cosmiano,

　　ludat cum pueris, amet puellas,

　　nec per circuitus loquatur illam,

　　ex qua nascimur, omnium parentem,

10　quam sanctus Numa mentulam vocabat.

　　versus hos tamen esse tu memento

　　Saturnalicios, Apollinaris:

　　mores non habet hic meos libellus.

11.70

　　Vendere, Tucca, potes centenis milibus emptos?

　　　　plorantis dominos vendere, Tucca, potes?

　　nec te blanditiae, nec verba rudesve querelae,

　　　　nec te dente tuo saucia colla movent?

5　ah facinus! tunica patet inguen utrimque levata,

　　　　inspiciturque tua mentula facta manu.

　　si te delectat numerata pecunia, vende

　　　　argentum, mensas, murrina, rura, domum;

　　vende senes servos—ignoscent—vende paternos.

10　ne pueros vendas, omnia vende miser.

　　luxuria est emere hos—quis enim dubitatve negatve?—

　　　　sed multo maior vendere luxuria est.

11.77

　　In omnibus Vacerra quod conclavibus

　　consumit horas et die toto sedet,

　　cenaturit Vacerra, non cacaturit.

❧ *Book 12*

12.3

Quod Flacco Varioque fuit summoque Maroni
    Maecenas, atavis regibus ortus eques,
gentibus et populis hoc te mihi, Prisce Terenti,
    fama fuisse loquax chartaque dicet anus.
5   tu facis ingenium, tu, si quid posse videmur;
    tu das ingenuae ius mihi pigritiae.
macte animi, quem rarus habes, morumque tuorum,
    quos Numa, quos hilaris possit habere Cato.
largiri, praestare, breves extendere census,
10   et dare quae faciles vix tribuere dei,
nunc licet et fas est. sed tu sub principe duro
    temporibusque malis ausus es esse bonus.

12.20

Quare non habeat, Fabulle, quaeris
uxorem Themison? habet sororem.

12.23

Dentibus atque comis—nec te pudet—uteris emptis.
    quid facies oculo, Laelia? non emitur.

12.68

Matutine cliens, urbis mihi causa relictae:
    atria, si sapias, ambitiosa colas.
non sum ego causidicus, nec amaris litibus aptus,
    sed piger et senior Pieridumque comes;
5   otia me somnusque iuvant, quae magna negavit
      Roma mihi. redeo, si vigilatur et hic.

12.90

Pro sene, sed clare, votum Maro fecit amico,
    cui gravis et fervens hemitritaeos erat,
si Stygias aeger non esset missus ad umbras,
    ut caderet magno victima grata Iovi.
5   coeperunt certam medici spondere salutem.
      ne votum solvat, nunc Maro vota facit.

12.91

Communis tibi cum viro, Magulla,
cum sit lectulus et sit exoletus,
quare dic mihi non sit et minister.
suspiras. ratio est, times lagonam.

12.92

Saepe rogare soles qualis sim, Prisce, futurus,
    si fiam locuples simque repente potens.
quemquam posse putas mores narrare futuros?
    dic mihi: si fias tu leo, qualis eris?

12.93

Qua moechum ratione basiaret
coram coniuge repperit Fabulla.
parvum basiat usque morionem;
hunc multis rapit osculis madentem
5   moechus protinus, et suis repletum
ridenti dominae statim remittit.
quanto morio maior est maritus!

☙ *Book 13*

13.3

Omnis in hoc gracili *Xeniorum* turba libello
    constabit nummis quattuor empta tibi.
quattuor est nimium? poterit constare duobus,
    et faciat lucrum bibliopola Tryphon.
5   haec licet hospitibus pro munere disticha mittas,
    si tibi tam rarus quam mihi nummus erit.
addita per titulos sua nomina rebus habebis;
    praetereas, si quid non facit ad stomachum.

13.4

Tus

Serus ut aetheriae Germanicus imperet aulae
    utque diu terris, da pia tura Iovi.

13.14

Lactucae

Cludere quae cenas lactuca solebat avorum,
    dic mihi, cur nostras inchoat illa dapes?

13.29

Vas Damascenorum

Pruna peregrinae carie rugosa senectae
    sume: solent duri solvere ventris onus.

13.63

Capones

Ne nimis exhausto macresceret inguine gallus,
    amisit testes. nunc mihi gallus erit.

13.74

Anseres

Haec servavit avis Tarpei templa Tonantis.
    miraris? nondum fecerat illa deus.

13.82

Ostrea

Ebria Baiano veni modo concha Lucrino.
    nobile nunc sitio luxuriosa garum.

13.108

Mulsum

Attica nectareum turbatis mella Falernum.
   misceri decet hoc a Ganymede merum.

☙ Book 14

14.73

Psittacus

Psittacus a vobis aliorum nomina discam.
   hoc didici per me dicere: "Caesar have."

14.134

Fascia pectoralis

Fascia, crescentes dominae compesce papillas,
   ut sit quod capiat nostra tegatque manus.

14.188

Cicero in membranis

Si comes ista tibi fuerit membrana, putato
   carpere te longas cum Cicerone vias.

14.189

Monobiblos Properti

Cynthia—facundi carmen iuvenale Properti—
   accepit famam, non minus ipsa dedit.

14.190

Titus Livius in membranis

Pellibus exiguis artatur Livius ingens,
    quem mea non totum bibliotheca capit.

14.191

Sallustius

Hic erit, ut perhibent doctorum corda virorum,
    primus Romana Crispus in historia.

14.194

Lucanus

Sunt quidam qui me dicant non esse poetam;
    sed qui me vendit bibliopola putat.

14.195

Catullus

Tantum magna suo debet Verona Catullo
    quantum parva suo Mantua Vergilio.

14.198

Catella Gallicana

Delicias parvae si vis audire catellae,
    narranti brevis est pagina tota mihi.

14.199

Asturco

Hic brevis ad numeros rapidum qui colligit unguem,
  venit ab auriferis gentibus Astur equus.

14.200

Canis vertragus

Non sibi sed domino venatur vertragus acer,
  inlaesum leporem qui tibi dente feret.

14.203

Puella Gaditana

Tam tremulum crisat, tam blandum prurit, ut ipsum
  masturbatorem fecerit Hippolytum.

14.204

Cymbala

Aera Celaenaeos lugentia matris amores
  esuriens gallus vendere saepe solet.

14.205

Puer

Sit nobis aetate puer, non pumice levis,
  propter quem placeat nulla puella mihi.

Commentary

ᴓ *Liber spectaculorum*

spect. 1

1   **barbara** usually understood as f. nom. sing. modifying *Memphis*, since the technique of framing a line with an adj.-noun pair is common in Latin poetry in general and Martial in particular (cf. *Assyrius . . . labor* in the following line). But, in an ambiguity that is likewise fairly common, the adj. might also be n. acc. pl., modifying *miracula*. Regardless of which noun the adj. modifies, it sounds an opening note of ethnocentrism that is especially striking in connection with so ancient a civilization as that of Egypt, among whose most admired accomplishments are precisely the pyramids. Although Latin *barbarus* does not always have the same tone as its English derivatives "barbaric" and "barbarian," its connotations are negative.

pyramidum This reference to the pyramids along the Nile begins a catalogue of architectural marvels constituting the Seven Wonders of the Ancient World.

sileat This is the first of a series of jussive subjunctives referring to earlier, non-Roman architectural achievements and expressing the idea of boasting or praising or, by contrast, keeping quiet (*iactet, laudentur, dissimulet, laudibus . . . ferant*). In the final verse comes the fut. indicative *loquetur*, referring to the new Amphitheater.

Memphis An ancient city on the Nile, founded as early as 3000 BCE, capital of the Old Kingdom and famous among Greeks and Romans. The complex of pyramids at Giza, including the celebrated Great Pyramid of Cheops/Khufu, is located nearby.

2   **Babylona** the ancient city on the Euphrates River, likewise dating back as early as 3000 BCE. Two of the Seven Wonders (the double set of city walls and the hanging gardens of Nebuchadnezzar) were found there, and Martial seems to be alluding to them both: if so, the epigram assigns to the newly built Flavian Amphitheater, dedicated by the emperor Titus in 80 CE, the status of seventh on the list.

3   **Triviae** an epithet of the Roman goddess Diana, assimilated to the Greek Artemis, whose cult was associated among other things with crossroads. The Temple of Artemis at Ephesus, in an area of Asia Minor inhabited in antiquity by Ionian Greeks, was another one of the Seven Wonders.

templo abl. of cause

molles There is a long tradition in Roman literature of stereotyping Greeks in general and Ionians in particular as soft, luxurious, effeminate, in contrast to hard, austere, manly Romans.

4   **dissimulet** "keep quiet, hide" i.e., may the Altar of Horns no longer bring Delos fame

Delon a small island in the Aegean famous for its sanctuary of Apollo and numerous other shrines and temples, including the altar mentioned here, made exclusively of animal horns with no mortar or other binding elements. It is described as one of the Seven Wonders by Martial's contemporary Plutarch (*Moralia* 983E) but otherwise does not appear on lists of the Seven Wonders, whose contents vary. Since the altar was said to have been constructed by Apollo himself, this couplet evokes Artemis in its first line (3), her brother in its second (4).

5   **aëre . . . vacuo pendentia** lit., "hanging in the empty sky," i.e., the structure was so tall that it seemed to be suspended in mid-air. The first word scans *ā-ĕrĕ*.

Mausolea poetic pl., referring to the monumental tomb of Mausolos, fourth-century BCE king of Caria, at Halicarnassus in Asia Minor; scanned *Māū-sō-lē-ă*.

7 An example of what in English-language scholarship has come to be called the "golden line": abVAB, where *a* and *b* are adjs. modifying the nouns *A* and *B*, and *V* is a verb. The elegance of the structure adds emphasis to the point.

Caesareo adj. equivalent to a dependent gen. ("the Caesarian amphitheater" = "Caesar's amphitheater"). *Caesar*, the cognomen of Julius Caesar and thus also of his adopted son Octavian (Augustus), was subsequently used by Roman emperors as a title, and later inspired such titles as *Kaiser* and *Czar*.

8 **unum pro cunctis** The juxtaposition emphasizes the contrast between this single structure and all the earlier architectural achievements that have just been listed; the Amphitheater will take the place of all other six! At this point Martial's epigram takes on the form known as the priamel: a list of several items builds up to the conclusion that none of them can compare to X (a common type is "some say . . . some say . . . but I say . . .").

Fig. 1. The Flavian Amphitheater ("Colosseum") in Rome. The pedestrians in this photograph give a good sense of the scale. Photograph by Paul Zangara / Wikimedia Commons.

spect. 2

1   **hic ubi** Anchoring an epigram in a specific person or place is a
    common opening technique in Martial. In this case it begins a
    series of temporal and visual contrasts between what is *now* to
    be seen in this part of the Rome and what was *previously* there
    (*hic ubi* again in 5 and 7, *ubi* in 9).

    sidereus . . . colossus Borrowed from Greek, the noun *colossus*
    denotes an impressively larger than life statue; most famous was
    the Colossos of Rhodes, a third-century BCE bronze statue of the
    sun-god more than 100 feet tall, regularly included in lists of the
    Seven Wonders. The reference here, however, is to the monu-
    mental statue of Nero in Rome, near the site on which the Fla-
    vian Amphitheater was later built, rededicated to the Sun after
    Nero's death; it was because of the proximity to this statue that
    the Flavian Amphitheater came in the Middle Ages to be known
    as the "Colosseum." Note the emphatic qualities of this line: the
    adj. *sidereus*, the noun *colossus*, the exaggerated statement that
    the statue is close to the stars, and the repetition with variation
    (adj. *sidereus* ~ noun *astra*).

2   **media pegmata celsa via** Note the word order (the meter shows
    which adj. modifies which noun); *pegmata* probably refers to
    scaffolding erected for the Arch of Titus, which spans the Via
    Sacra and was under construction when the Flavian Amphi-
    theater was dedicated.

3   Another "golden line" (cf. spect. 1.7); *feri . . . regis* refers to the
    emperor Nero in a highly disparaging way. The negative asso-
    ciations of the title *rex* at Rome should never be underestimated:
    after the last of seven kings was expelled and the Republic es-
    tablished in the late sixth century BCE, Rome never again had a
    rex. Julius Caesar's enemies capitalized on the fear that he was
    secretly aiming to become king; after him, emperors were called
    princeps and *imperator*, but not even Domitian (who wished to
    be addressed as *dominus et deus*) claimed the title *rex*.

    radiabant atria The verb suggests the gleaming of marble and
    gold, and the noun refers to Nero's Domus Aurea, a massive pal-

ace occupying about 125 acres of the area between the Palatine and Esquiline hills, constructed after the devastating fire of 64 CE. As this poem reminds its readers, after Nero's death in 68 CE much of the Domus Aurea was put to new uses.

4   Note the rhetorical contrasts shaping this line (*una* vs. *tota, urbe* vs. *domus*); *tota . . . in urbe* is of course hyperbolic.

5   **venerabilis** modifies *moles* in the next line

6   **stagna Neronis** The Domus Aurea included an artificial lake, which was subsequently filled in and became the site of the Flavian Amphitheater.

7   **velocia munera** "gifts [to the Roman public] that were quickly erected"; in apposition to *thermas*. The Baths of Titus on the Oppian hill became a standard fixture on the urban landscape of Rome. Elsewhere Martial uses the phrase "the three baths" (*triplices thermae*, 10.51.12) to refer to those of Agrippa, Nero, and Titus.

8   **miseris** dat. of disadvantage; translate "from." The adj. expresses sympathy for those Romans whose homes had been torn down to make way for Nero's palace.

   superbus ager i.e., the land claimed by a man who was *superbus* (transferred epithet); the effect approaches that of personification. The indirect description of Nero as *superbus* contributes to his portrayal as a tyrant: the last Roman king was called Tarquinius Superbus.

9   **Claudia . . . porticus** i.e., the Portico of Claudius on the Caelian hill, near a temple dedicated to the deified emperor

   diffusas . . . explicat umbras lit., "unfolds its scattered shadows," i.e., spreads ample shade over a large area; the pple. functions as a proleptic adj.

10 **deficientis** "at its farthest end"; pleonastic with *ultima pars*

11 **te praeside** abl. absolute, a flattering remark that continues the contrast between past and present, in this case between Nero and the current emperor Titus, who is neither a *ferus rex* nor *superbus* but a guardian of the people. For *Caesar* cf. spect. 1.7.

12   The final line brings the point home with yet another formu-
     lation of the central contrast: whereas Nero, in the role of *do-*
     minus, had built a massive complex for his own pleasure, Titus
     and before him his father Vespasian have made this part of the
     city available to the public (*populi* evokes the traditional phrase
     populus Romanus).

spect. 7

1   **qualiter** correlates with *sic* in line 3

     Prometheus His story is most famously told in Hesiod's *Theogo-*
     ny and the play *Prometheus Bound* attributed to Aeschylus. Hav-
     ing attempted to trick Zeus by giving human beings the secret of
     fire, Prometheus received a dire punishment: he was chained to
     a cliff in the Caucasus region (*Scythica . . . rupe*) and a giant eagle
     came every day to eat out his liver, which grew back every night.

2   The juxtaposition of *adsiduam* and *nimio* emphasizes the horror
     of Prometheus' punishment: the bird kept coming back for more,
     his entrails never ran out. The verb *pavit*, too, adds a gruesome
     touch: Prometheus was "feeding" the bird against his will.

3   **Caledonio . . . urso** Caledonia (northern Scotland) lay at the
     northern edge of the world known to the Romans. Their armies
     did not establish a more or less stable presence until 83–84 CE at
     the earliest, but Romans had almost certainly been trading with
     the peoples of Caledonia for some time.

4   **non falsa . . . in cruce** i.e., a real cross, as opposed to a stage
     prop (see on *Laureolus*). Crucifixion was a means of publicly
     torturing and killing slaves and condemned criminals, and was
     a major feature of the Roman cultural and linguistic landscape.
     Slaves in Plautine comedies are routinely insulted, for example,
     with phrases like *i in malam crucem*.

     Laureolus A character in a mime play of the same name com-
     posed by a certain Catullus (not the well-known first-century
     BCE poet) and staged for the first time in 41 CE, Laureolus was
     a runaway slave who led a band of thieves and was eventually

punished by being crucified; his death was staged in a famously gory scene. Martial's epigram refers to a spectacle in the Flavian Amphitheater—perhaps staged as part of an opening celebration—in which a man was hung from a cross and torn apart by a bear, thus becoming a real-life Laureolus. Public spectacles in which people and animals were tortured or killed were not uncommon in Rome, and these were sometimes staged as mythological scenes. Martial elsewhere alludes to a re-enactment of the story of Pasiphae and the bull (spect. 5).

5   **laceri membris stillantibus artus** Note the chiastic word order; the pple. means "dripping with blood."

6   **inque omni nusquam corpore corpus erat** Note the paradoxical thought as well as the polyptoton (juxtaposition of two forms of the same noun). The gory detail and rhetorical flourish are typical of Latin literature of the first century CE.

7   The manuscripts containing this poem give the incomplete line *denique supplicium*; various ways of filling out the line have been suggested, including *dignus* (or *dignum* or *merito*) *tulit: ille parentis* (deriving from the nineteenth-century scholar Schneidewin) and more recently *meruit quo crimine tantum?* (Holford-Stevens, adopted by Coleman). All these suggestions include the idea that the man deserved his punishment: in that case the poem has even more disturbing implications, since the options listed below (*vel . . . vel . . . vel . . .*) suggest that Martial does not actually know what this man was condemned for.

8   **domini iugulum foderat ense** i.e., he was a slave who had killed his master

9   **arcano . . . auro** abl. of separation with the verb *spoliaverat* ("or else he had stripped temples of their hidden treasures of gold")

10   **subdiderat . . . faces** i.e., had set fire to. Precisely this accusation had been made of Nero in connection with the catastrophic fire that swept over the city of Rome in 64 CE.

      tibi, Roma The apostrophe to the city of Rome adds variety to the syntax and intensity to the pathos.

12 **in quo** "in whose case"

quae fuerat fabula i.e., *id quod fabula fuerat*, with the antecedent omitted and the rel. pron. agreeing in gender with the predicate noun *fabula*. The noun refers to the mythic "tale" of Prometheus' fate and perhaps also to the "play" dramatizing Laureolus' crucifixion; in any case it is contrasted with the all-too-real punishment (*poena*) to which this man has been subjected.

❧ Book 1

1.1

METER: Phalaecian hendecasyllable

1 **hic** m. nom. sing. *hic* rather than the adv. *hīc* but, as usual in Latin verse, the syllable counts as long. The demonstrative might refer to a portrait of the author placed at the beginning of the original manuscript, but it has also been suggested that the phrase *hic est* echoes what someone would say when catching sight of a famous man on the street.

quem legis . . . quem requiris Note how Martial immediately draws the anonymous reader—you—in, and how the combination of these two second-person forms with the demonstratives *hic* and *ille* immediately puts "you" into a relationship with "him."

ille hyperbaton, take with *Martialis* ("this is that famous man, Martial . . .")

2 **toto notus in orbe** In Greek and Roman culture, it was not considered unacceptably arrogant to boast of one's own fame, especially if the claim was arguably true. Still, even allowing for the possibility of self-advertising hyperbole, there is something puzzling about Martial's claim. His previous publications—the *Liber spectaculorum* of 80 CE and the *Xenia* and the *Apophoreta* of 84–85 CE—were probably not sufficient to give Martial anything approaching worldwide fame by 86 CE, the year Book 1 was first published. Perhaps Martial had become well known, thanks

to informal recitations of his poetry and the circulation of small collections. Another possibility is that this poem was not a part of the first edition of Book 1 but written for a later, second edition of Martial's epigrams: see discussion in the Introduction.

Martialis In a traditional technique often designated with the Greek word *sphragis* ("seal"), an ancient poet might place his name at the end of a collection of poems in order to mark it as his. Here, as Ovid had done with his *Amores,* Martial places his seal on the beginning of the book.

3   **argutis** Martial claims a number of formal qualities for his epigrams that are characteristic of the tradition in Greek and Latin poetry known as Alexandrian: brevity, refinement, elegance, delicacy. But he also claims the right to use blunt, coarse language when appropriate; the combination is emblematic of the variety and liveliness of the genre.

epigrammaton gen. pl. (ἐπιγραμμάτων). The Greek borrowing *epigramma* appears sometimes with Latin endings (3rd declension gen. sing. *-is,* gen. pl. *-um*), sometimes with Greek endings (gen. sing. *-os,* gen. pl. *-ōn*).

libellis Martial frequently uses this noun, the diminutive of *libri,* to describe his poetry, one of many ways in which he follows in the footsteps of Catullus (cf. Catullus 1.1: *cui dono lepidum novum libellum?*). The diminutive may be appealing to the aesthetic of brevity characteristic of the genre, referring to the practice of circulating small collections of epigrams before publishing the larger books we now have, or both.

4   **cui** the rel. pron., its antecedent being *Martialis*

lector studiose The adj. suggests both "studious" and "enthusiastic." See the Introduction for discussion of Martial and his reader.

quod dedisti understand *id* as antecedent of *quod.* As becomes clear two lines later, this clause functions as the direct object of *habent*: "only a few poets, after they are dead, have that which you have given me while I am still alive."

5   **viventi . . . atque sentienti** modifying *cui*. The second pple. expands upon the first, the notion being that the dead no longer perceive anything (cf. Anna's words to Dido at Vergil *Aeneid* 4.34: *id cinerem aut manis credis curare sepultos?*). This was only one of many different understandings of death and the afterlife current in antiquity.

6   **post cineres** i.e., after their bodies have been cremated, a compressed way of saying "after they are dead." Martial's boast that he has already achieved renown in the here and now stands in bold contrast with the more traditional poetic claim on lasting fame *after* death.

1.2

1   **qui . . . cupis** "you who wish . . ." Once again you, Martial's reader, are addressed at the poem's beginning. Note the elaborate order in this poem's first line, as if advertising one of the aesthetic pleasures that awaits us: the words *qui . . . cupis . . . meos . . . libellos* are interlocked with *tecum . . . esse . . . ubicumque*.

2   **comites longae . . . viae** Here and elsewhere Martial gives us a valuable glimpse at reading practices among some Romans: they might take books with them on long journeys. In one epigram (11.3) Martial boasts that people living in Britain and centurions stationed in Romania have copies of his poetry.

3   **hos** sc. *libellos.* Martial is contrasting *this* edition—in a compact format known as the codex, a book consisting of relatively small bound pages (*brevibus . . . tabellis*) made of animal-skin parchment (*membrana*) and thus not unlike a modern paperback edition—with the more usual format of a larger and more cumbersome scroll made of papyrus, which was stored in a case called a *scrinium*. It has been argued with some plausibility that this poem, like 1.1, was composed *after* the initial papyrus-scroll publication of Book 1 in order to mark a second edition in the less usual codex format.

4   **magnis** understand *poetis* and/or *libellis*; contrasted with *me* just as *scrinia* is contrasted with *manus una* (cf. 9.praef.7: *maiores maiora sonent, mihi parva locuto . . .*). In other words, it takes a whole *scrinium* to hold "the heavies," whereas I can fit in the palm of a hand. Once again we see the aesthetic of the small, refined, and light. *Me* and *ubi sim venalis* can be understood as the voice of the poet Martial, identifying himself with his work in a common figure of speech ("we will read some Shakespeare" = "we will read some of Shakespeare's poetry"), or else as the voice of the personified book itself.

5   **ne . . . ignores** purpose clause

    ubi sim venalis Does this phrase suggest that the poet and/or his work can be compared to a slave or prostitute? See the next poem.

7–8 The poem ends with a technique characteristic of the Latin literary tradition: anchoring texts in specific places in the urban landscape of Rome. With its emphasis on *itself* as an object that can be bought and sold, this poem expresses a theme that is in general more characteristic of Latin than of Greek literature.

7   **libertum docti Lucensis . . . Secundum** The line-framing technique here creates a chiastically arranged phrase identifying the bookseller. We know nothing about these two men other than what this poem tells us. *Bibliopolae* like Secundus would pay the author for his manuscript and then have their scribes make copies to be sold for profit. It is not clear whether the author received any percentage, but Martial repeatedly makes the point that he cannot make a living from his poetry alone.

8   **limina post Pacis** = *post limina Pacis*; as often in Latin poetry, the prep. comes after its object. The reference is to the architectural complex of porticoes and gardens surrounding the Templum Pacis, dedicated by Vespasian in 75 CE to commemorate his victory in Judaea and to house the spoils from Jerusalem.

    Palladiumque forum Begun under Domitian or perhaps even Vespasian, this was located between the Forum of Augustus and the Templum Pacis, and is more commonly known as the

Forum Transitorium (because the road known as the Argiletum passed through it) or the Forum of Nerva (the later emper-
or who formally dedicated it in 97 CE). Martial's phrase refers to
the fact that the forum was dominated by a temple to Minerva,
identified with the Greek goddess Athena, one of whose epithets was Pallas.

1.3

1   **Argiletanas . . . tabernas** The Argiletum was a major street in
Rome, leading up from the Forum Romanum into the district
known as the Subura. In view of the Subura's reputation—hec-
tic, eclectic, and sometimes seedy—Martial's phrase suggests
not only bookshops like Lucensis', located at the beginning of
the Argiletum (cf. 1.2.7), but also bars and brothels. A possible
implication of the preceding poem is here explored more openly: that the book is like a slave or prostitute who sells himself.
Martial seems to have been inspired by Horace, *Epistles* 1.20,
where the poet likewise addresses his book, personifying it as a
slave who is putting himself on the market.

  mavis habitare Whereas in the preceding poem Martial's poetry book was fleetingly given a voice (*me manus una capit; ubi
sim venalis*), here it is now fully personified.

2   **parve liber** cf. 1.1.3 (*libellis*). The adj. *parvus* may add a pathetic
tone, as if Martial were addressing an innocent child or inexperienced slave: "you poor, clueless little book."

  vacent "have room for you"; subjunctive with *cum* in concessive
sense

3   **nescis, heu, nescis** The repetition of the verb and the interjection *heu* create a (melo-) dramatic tone.

  dominae fastidia Romae The ABA word order is typical of literary Latin of all kinds, prose and verse. Referring to Rome as
domina simultaneously evokes a long tradition of imperialistic
imagery (cf. Vergil *Aeneid* 1.282, *Romanos rerum dominos gen-
temque togatam*) and plays into Martial's technique of personi-

fication: if his book is an inexperienced young slave, Rome is a grand lady and will be a demanding mistress.

4   **Martia turba** Since Rome was founded by Romulus, son of Mars, the adj. *Martius, -a, -um* can refer to the city or its people. Martial's phrase is thus a poetic equivalent of *populus Romanus.*

5   **rhonchi** with ellipsis of verb (*sunt*); the noun refers to snorts as an expression of dismissal or disdain. The physical imagery is continued with *nasum rhinocerotis* in the next line.

    iuvenesque senesque / et pueri Although Martial repeatedly makes it clear that his readership consists of both men and women, here he refers to the three phases of a man's life (a *puer* until he grows his full beard, a *iuvenis* until about the age of forty, and thereafter a *senex*) in order to make the point that this attitude is shared by readers of all ages.

7   **audieris** alternative form of *audiveris*, fut. pf. indicative act. This line personifies the book as a successful performer being acclaimed by an adoring audience who shout "bravo!" (Greek *sophōs*) as he throws them kisses (cf. Phaedrus *Fabulae* 5.7.28–29, *iactat basia / tibicen,* describing a fluteplayer who mistakenly thinks the audience is greeting him upon his return to the stage after he broke a leg). The next line comes as a brutal contrast.

8   **ibis . . . in astra** The language is hyperbolic and ironically suggests traditional imagery for glory (cf. Vergil *Aeneid* 1.287, *famam qui terminet astris*) even as it imagines a moment of humiliating rejection.

    ab excusso missus . . . sago This refers to the practice of tossing someone in the air from a blanket or cloak as a way of teasing, mocking, or tormenting him. A note from Peter Howell's commentary is worth citing: "At Eton, in the days when, in accordance with old public school tradition, thoughtless brutality was combined with close familiarity with Latin texts, this line of Martial used to be shouted out while unfortunate new boys were tossed in blankets."

9   **domini** echoing *dominae . . . Romae* in line 3, this refers to Martial himself: if the book is a slave, the poet is his master.

     ne . . . patiare lituras The noun refers to the erasure of stylus marks made in wax tablets, or to the use of a sponge to wipe ink off papyrus or parchment. This brings us back to the physical realities of the book: this slave boy fears not his master's whip or fist, but his eraser. The imagery continues in the following line.

10   **lusus . . . tuos** The book just wants to have fun and thus wishes to avoid his master's "severe pen" (*tristis harundo*).

11   **aetherias . . . volitare per auras** the adj.-noun line-framing technique. The language is elevated, perhaps echoing Vergil's phrase *virum volitare per ora* (*Georgics* 3.9) and Ennius' *volito vivos per ora virum* (*Varia* 18), asserting the immortality of epic poets. The juxtaposition with *lascive* ("you naughty boy") reminds us, however, that we are reading epigram, not epic.

12   **poteras tutior esse** "you could have been safer"; the impf. and plpf. indicative of the verbs *sum* and *possum* are often used where we might expect a subjunctive (here in a contrafactual statement).

1.6

1   **aetherias . . . per auras** The same phrase, in the same metrical position, is found at 1.3.11. Martial frequently reuses words, phrases, and images.

     aquila . . . portante abl. absolute, enclosing the direct object of the pple. (*puerum*); the phrase is itself enclosed within the line-framing *aetherias . . . per auras*. The entire line thus has the form ABCBA, embracing the boy in its midst.

     puerum Even though he is never named in this poem, Roman readers would have easily recognized the reference to the beautiful young Trojan prince Ganymede, carried off by Jupiter's eagle to be the god's cupbearer and concubine. Ganymede and the eagle are a common theme in Roman art, depicted in media ranging from mosaics to wall-painting to statuary and even jewelry.

Fig. 2. A 3rd-century CE mosaic depicting Ganymede being carried by Jupiter's eagle. From a Roman villa near Bignor, West Sussex, England. Photograph by Craig Williams.

2   **timidis unguibus** The eagle is afraid of hurting Ganymede and so, in a rhetorically colored phrase that verges on transferred epithet, his talons are described as "timid."

3   **nunc** creates a contrast between the scene just described, which took place in the mythic past (*haesit,* pf. tense), and what is happening in Martial's own day (*exorat* and *ludit,* pres. tense): a spectacle in the arena in which hares frolic unharmed in lions' mouths. Book 1 contains a "cycle" of seven epigrams on this incident that use it as the occasion for flattering the emperor Domitian: like the lion, he is mighty but shows mercy.

exorat The verb refers to the act of convincing someone by begging or pleading (*orare*), i.e., with words; cf. Servius ad *Aen.* 3.370: *orare est petere, exorare impetrare.* To make a hare its subject and a lion its object is to anthropomorphize.

Caesareos cf. spect.1.7.

5   **quae maiora putas miracula?** *quae* is the interrog. adj., modify-
     ing *miracula*, and *putas* introduces an indirect statement, with
     the infinitive *esse*, as often, understood. Either this question is
     being posed to an anonymous reader (cf. *legis* and *requiris* in 1.1,
     addressed to *lector studiose*) or else this is a generalizing second
     person sing. (cf. Vergil *Aeneid* 4.401: *migrantis* <u>*cernas*</u> *totaque ex
     urbe ruentis*).

     utrisque / . . . adest dat. of possession: "each [of the two] has . . ."

6   **haec . . . illa** sc. *miracula,* referring to the scenes described in the
     second and first couplet respectively

1.10

METER: Scazon

1   Since the preface to Book 1 announces the principle that, unlike
     such earlier poets as Catullus, Martial will not use real names
     when attacking or insulting people, *Gemellus* and *Maronilla*
     are pseudonyms for real people whom the poet knew, wholly
     invented characters, or a mixture of both. Martial never uses
     these two names again.

2   The entire line consists of a rapid series of verbs breathlessly
     linked by repetitions of *et.*

3-4 The question-and-answer format is repeated in two successive
     lines, creating a lively tone: it is as if we were listening to a fast-
     paced dialogue.

4   **tussit** The final word comes as a surprise and at the same time
     delivers the epigram's sharp point: Maronilla's cough suggests
     that she is sick, firing Gemellus' imagination with the prospect
     of becoming a wealthy widower. The practice of legacy-hunting
     (*captatio*) is a recurring theme not only in Martial's epigrams
     but in Petronius' *Satyricon*, Juvenal's satires and other Latin
     texts, as is the other side of the coin: older men and women ma-
     nipulating their suitors by holding out the hope of being written
     into their wills (cf. 2.26).

1.13

1   The structure of this verse (abCAB) is a variation on the "golden line" in which C is not a verb but the clause *gladium cum traderet.*

casta along with *pudica,* a traditional term of high praise for a *matrona* or married lady

Arria Arria Maior, wife of Caecina *Paetus*, who was condemned to death in 42 CE after a failed conspiracy against the emperor Claudius. Like most upper-class men in his situation, Paetus was given the option of committing suicide and thus meeting a death far more honorable than execution. Arria not only decided to join her husband in death but took the first step, thus becoming a paradigmatic example not only of the courageous woman but of the wife so dedicated to her husband that she *chooses* to join him in death (as far as we can tell, Arria herself had not been condemned). In the better known version of Arria's death narrated by Pliny (*Epistulae* 3.16), she stabs herself and hands her husband the sword with the words: *Paete, non dolet.* Martial here gives us a variation on the theme.

2   **quem** the antecedent is *gladium*

3   **si qua fides** As usual after *si, nisi, num,* and *ne, qua* is used instead of *aliqua*; understand *est mihi*, i.e., "trust me."

4   **tu quod facies** i.e., *id quod tu facies*

hoc refers back to the entire clause *tu quod facies*: the pron. is not strictly necessary but underscores the contrast between Arria's wound, already inflicted (*vulnus quod feci*), and Paetus', which is soon to come (*tu quod facies*).

1.15

1   **mihi** dat. of agent with the gerundive *memorande*; like many in Martial, this line has an Ovidian feel (cf. Ovid *Tristia* 1.5.1: *o mihi post ullos numquam memorande sodales*).

Iuli The epigram tells us all we need to know about this man, at least for a first reading: Julius is one of Martial's best friends and is about to mark his sixtieth birthday. An experienced reader of Martial's poetry may conclude that the man being addressed here is Julius Martialis, a longtime friend of the poet who appears in every one of the twelve numbered books of epigrams (their friendship thus lasted at least thirty-four years) and is often the addressee in thoughtful poems like this one; Book 6 is dedicated to him. The fact that the poet and he have the same cognomen is almost certainly coincidental.

2 **fides** Etymologically related to *foedus* (a bond or agreement that joins two parties), *fides* is an ideal of fundamental importance to Roman culture, and has a particularly close association with friendship or *amicitia*.

cana iura As often, the adj. is metaphorical ("ancient, venerable") rather than literal ("white-haired"); the noun reinforces the imagery of *fides*. A friendship of long standing brings with it certain rights and privileges, in this case the right to speak frankly and give blunt advice.

3 **bis . . . tricensimus** Paraphrasing numbers in this way ("twice thirtieth" for "sixtieth") is a common stylistic feature of Latin literature.

consul Since every year had a unique pair of consuls who took office on January 1st, a standard way of identifying a specific year was to name the two consuls in the abl. absolute; thus an event in 63 BCE could be described as having occurred *M. Tullio Cicerone et C. Antonio Hybrida consulibus*. Here we see a related usage: a metonymy by which the noun *consul* signifies a year.

4 **et** here in a strongly contrastive sense, "and yet." What Martial means by the paradoxical remark that his friend is nearly sixty years old but has barely lived a few days will become clear by the end of the poem.

5 **non bene distuleris** lit., "you will not have postponed well," i.e., it is not good to postpone

videas quae i.e., *ea quae videas*; rel. clause of characteristic

negari i.e., *tibi*; things that can be withheld from or even taken away from you

6   **solum hoc** explained in the following clause (*quod fuit*, i.e., *id quod fuit*)

    ducas As often, a second person jussive subjunctive expresses an imperative. The verb, here in the sense "think, consider," is followed by an indirect statement (acc. *hoc* + infinitive *esse*).

7   **curaeque catenatique labores** The pairing of *-que* is common in poetic Latin, where *A-que B-que* often means not "both A and B" but simply "A and B." The image of *catenati labores* is that of a series of hardships, one chained to the other to form a long line, or else the phrase evokes the image of a chain gang of slaves shackled one to the other.

8   **fugitiva** perhaps continuing the imagery of slaves, since *fugitivus* was the standard term to denote a runaway slave

9   **haec** i.e., *gaudia*

    utraque manu . . . adsere playing on the technical term *manu adserere*, referring to the symbolic gesture in a legal proceeding by means of which a man asserted that someone who claimed to be free was actually his slave

10 **fluunt . . . lapsa** As regularly in Latin, the combination of pf. pple. and finite verb describes two separate but related actions that in English are usually expressed by two separate finite verbs: "having slipped out, they fall away" = "they slip out and fall away"

    sic quoque "even so," i.e., even if you hold on to them tightly

11 **non est . . . sapientis** predicative gen.: "it does not belong to the wise man" or "it is not the mark of a wise man"

    vivam As the next line makes clear, this is fut. indicative, not pres. subjunctive.

1.16

1   The threefold anaphora of *sunt* underscores the tripartite qualitative division: good, middling, bad. Martial's poetry is marked by, and periodically claims for itself, variety in theme, language, metre, structure, length—and even quality.

2 **legis** Whereas we might at first understand the verb to be addressed to the anonymous reader (cf. 1.1), the vocative *Avite* in the line's second half shows that this is not the case. The addressee is probably L. Stertinius Avitus, a powerful friend and protector of Martial and himself also a poet (cf. 9.praef.). As usual in Martial's epigrams, however, readers may find meaning in this brief poem without knowing who Avitus is.

1.20

1 **turba spectante vocata** Since *vocare* can mean "to invite to dinner," the scene Martial is describing is that of a crowd of invited guests watching.

2 **solus** Emphatically placed at the beginning of the line, this communicates the main point: this man is eating all the fine mushrooms himself, not sharing them with his guests. Martial, Pliny, Seneca, Juvenal, and other Roman writers periodically complain of this and similar bad behavior on the part of hosts.

boletos a particularly prized type of mushroom

Caeciliane a pseudonym (cf. 1.10.1) that Martial uses throughout his collection, perhaps partially because of its convenient dactylic shape. It is hard to see a single, coherent character attached to the name, nor is it clear that we should expect to find one.

3 **tanto** modifies *ventre*; take *tibi* with *precabor*

4 According to some rumors at least, the emperor Claudius died after eating a mushroom poisoned by his wife, Agrippina the Younger, mother of the future emperor Nero. According to yet other rumors—vividly narrated by Tacitus in his *Annales*—Agrippina herself was eventually killed at the orders of her son.

edit, edas Note the emphatic juxtaposition of two different forms of the same verb, delivering the poem's humorously (?) aggressive point.

1.24

1   **aspicis . . . illum . . .?** A number of Martial's epigrams begin
with the question "do you see?" and/or a demonstrative ("that
man/woman who . . ."), an effective technique for quickly drawing the reader into a scenario.

incomptis . . . capillis In Roman terms, untidy, unkempt hair—
as opposed to a neatly curled or oiled coiffure—signifies a rough
masculinity.

Deciane Experienced readers of Martial may recognize the
name: a friend of Martial's, a Stoic and a lawyer who, like the
poet himself, came from Spain (cf. 2.5). This positioning of the
vocative of the addressee's name—in the second half of the first
line—is one of the most characteristic rhythmic techniques of
Martial's epigrams in elegiac couplets.

2   **cuius** like *qui* at the beginning of the next line, referring back to
illum

et ipse "even you yourself," alluding to Decianus' stern Stoicism

triste supercilium The adj., as often, means not "sad, unhappy"
but "grim, severe." The eyebrow was a common metaphor for
stern disapproval or haughtiness; cf. the English derivative *su-
percilious* and the phrase "to raise one's eyebrows at."

3   **Curios . . . Camillos** "generic" use of the pl. of a proper name to
mean "Curius, Camillus, and men like them." These are para-
gons of Roman masculinity, famous for their military accomplishments and exemplary austerity and severity. Manius Curius Dentatus (d. 270 BCE) was celebrated for his victories over the
Samnites and Sabines as well as King Pyrrhus; Marcus Furius
Camillus (d. ca. 365 BCE) was known as "savior of his country
and second founder of Rome" after vanquishing the Gauls who
had captured Rome in 390 BCE.

4   **nolito** the so-called fut. imperative, an alternative to *noli*. The
scansion is *nō-lĭ-tŏ*; the final *-ō* of verb forms is often shortened
in the poetry of Martial's era.

fronti Although the reference to unkempt hair draws attention to the literal meaning of this noun ("forehead"), it can also more generally refer to a person's "appearance." A similar semantic slide commonly occurs with the noun *os* ("mouth" > "face" > "expression").

nupsit With this single word the sharp point is driven home: the verb *nubo* refers to the role of the bride in a wedding ceremony (cf. *nubes,* "wedding veil"), whereas the groom's role is described as "leading a woman into matrimony" (*in matrimonium ducere*); cf. 8.12 below. Despite the appearance he gives of a stern, rough Roman masculinity, the unnamed man of Martial's epigram has just played a quintessentially feminine role. The contrast between appearance and reality is a recurring theme in Martial's poetry, and figures like this are frequent targets of his sharp and often gossipy wit. A number of ancient texts describe weddings between males at Rome, consistently representing the ceremonies in terms of sharply contrasted gender roles: a masculine groom takes a feminine male bride, and it is the latter who receives the brunt of the ridicule.

1.32

1 **amo** the final vowel is short (cf. 1.24.4)

Sabidi Martial uses the name in only one other poem of his entire collection, an epigram in the third book in which a man named Sabidius is mocked for his disgusting breath (3.17). The great majority of readers of this poem will not know that, however, and will read it for and by itself. Since the speaker gives no reason for his dislike of Sabidius, this epigram draws all the more attention to its cleverly crafted evocation of the experience of unexplainable but strong antipathy.

nec possum dicere quare At this point some readers may hear an echo of Catullus' famous monodistich 85 (*odi et amo. quare id faciam, fortasse requiris. / nescio, sed fieri sentio et excrucior*) and may then note the distance in tone and theme that separates the two poems.

2   **hoc tantum** "only this"

non amo te This monodistich thus begins and ends with the same words, a particularly compressed form of the technique known as ring composition. When the dean of Christ Church College in Oxford, Dr. John Fell, asked him to translate Martial's epigram as a condition for revoking an imminent explusion, the satirist Tom Brown (1663–1704) produced this version in rhyming iambs: "I do not love thee, Doctor Fell; / The reason why, I cannot tell. / But this I know, and know full well: / I do not love thee, Doctor Fell."

1.33

1   **amissum** a euphemistic reference to death

2   **si quis adest** in contrast with *cum sola est* in the preceding line. The absence of a connective draws attention to the contrast; the technique is known as adversative asyndeton.

iussae "on [her] command"

3   **non luget** The subject is expressed by the following clause, *quisquis . . . quaerit*.

Gellia Whereas the name was in the nom. sing. in line 1, here it is vocative sing. Such shifts are not uncommon in Martial's epigrams, in this case corresponding to a bipartite structure: 1–2 describe a situation, 3–4 express a response (see Introduction for further discussion).

4   Literally, "that man grieves truly who grieves without a witness," i.e., only someone who grieves when there is no one else around can truly be said to grieve. With this closing *sententia*—a brief, memorably worded statement of general applicability—the smoothly flowing poem comes to its end and we perceive a chiastic structure to the thought, developed line by line: Gellia does not weep when <u>alone</u> (1); she weeps in the presence of <u>others</u> (2); a general point about seeking the praise of <u>others</u> (3); a general point about mourning <u>alone</u> (4). Each line, moreover, uses a different word to refer to mourning, a variation characteristic of Martial's artistry: *flet* (1), *lacrimae* (2), *luget* (3), *dolet* (4).

1.34

1   **Lesbia** Especially since Martial prominently cites Catullus as one of his poetic models, the name is intriguing. Is this woman in any way like Catullus' beloved?

2   **peccas** It is almost always misleading to translate this verb "sin" when it occurs in a non-Christian text, since the English word has such strong religious associations. In classical Latin *peccare* denotes such things as "make a mistake, lose one's way, go astray"; describing a woman's sexual behavior, it usually suggests that she is a married woman having sexual relations with someone other than her husband, i.e., committing *adulterium*. The same is true of the vocabulary of thievery (*furta*). The implication that Lesbia is married becomes explicit in the next line (*adulter*).

3   **plus spectator . . . quam . . . adulter** In other words, Lesbia derives more pleasure from being watched than from the mere fact of being with her lover. Exhibitionism is the subject of several other epigrams by Martial and of Ovid's *Amores* 3.14 before him.

4   **gaudia si qua latent** lit., "delights, if any of them are hidden," i.e., "any delights which are hidden." For *qua*, see on 1.13.3.

5   **at** as usual, marks a stronger contrast than *sed*: "by contrast . . ." or "yet even . . ."

   veloque seraque cf. 1.15.7.

6   **raraque** nom. sing., modifying *rima*, which is the subject of *patet*; the conj. does not continue the sequence of *veloque seraque* but introduces a new clause. References to voyeurism in brothels and elsewhere (e.g., watching sexual scenes through keyholes, cracks in the wall, or even holes made for the purpose) are found in other epigrams by Martial, Petronius' *Satyricon* and other Latin texts.

   Submemmi fornice The noun *fornix, fornicis* literally means "archway, vault," but since city prostitutes sometimes met their customers under archways, the noun is also a metonymy for "brothel." Christian writers later used the verb *fornicari* and the nouns *fornicator, fornicatrix* and *fornicatio* to refer to a variety of sexual acts—not just prostitution—that they wished to condemn. *Submemmi* is gen. sing. either of the name of a brothel-owner (*Submemmius*) or of a district known for its brothels (*Submemmium*). The name appears only in Martial, who writes of foul *Submemmianae buccae* (11.61.2) and, presumably with irony, *Submemmianae uxores* (3.82.2).

7 **a Chione . . . vel ab Iade** The Greek names—"Snow" and "Violet" respectively—refer to prostitutes, as *lupas* in the next line makes clear. Martial uses "Chione" to refer to a prostitute in several other epigrams.

8 **abscondunt . . . et monumenta** i.e., even prostitutes who ply their trade amongst the tombs lining the roads leading in and out of Roman cities are discreet enough to meet their customers in the dark. Ancient graffiti containing sexual insults, at least one of them communicating that a man named Felix offered fellatio for a low price, have been found on tombs in the Porta Nocera necropolis outside the walls of Pompeii (*Corpus Inscriptionum Latinarum* 4.5408: *Felix fel(l)at as(se) I*; see also 5406, 10222, 10232).

lupas lit., "she-wolves," a colloquial term for female prostitutes, just as *lupanar* ("wolf's den") can signify a brothel. The adj. *spurcas* ("filthy") reminds us of a double standard: many Roman men were perfectly happy to pay for the services of prostitutes, and to do so was seen—even by moralists like Cicero and Cato—as entirely acceptable as long as it was not overdone, yet the prostitutes themselves were liable to insults like this.

9 **numquid** a somewhat stronger version of the interrog. particle *num*, posing a question in such a way as to imply that a negative answer is expected ("It certainly doesn't . . . does it?")

10 **deprendi . . . non futui** Both of these are pres. pass. infinitives and the latter is a primary obscenity, i.e., one of a small set of non-metaphorical words for sexual organs and acts whose use was prohibited in certain literary genres and whose appearance thus marked an utterance as coarse and direct (other primary

obscenities include *mentula, cunnus,* and *pedicare*). *Futui* has all the more impact here because it comes as the final word of this poem and is, moreover, the first occurrence of an obscene word in Book 1.

Lesbia In Martial's epigrams in elegiac couplets the vocative of the poem's addressee is not infrequently found in the second half of both the first and the last line, a variation on the technique of ring-composition that often has the effect of making the final verse more memorable or sententious.

1.35

METER: Phalaecian hendecasyllable

1   The first line of this poem comes as a direct response to the last line of the preceding poem. Some of Martial's poetry is "indecent" (*parum severos*) in language and imagery, and this epigram offers a justification—in the process using the second verbal obscenity of Book 1 (see line 5).

scribere me The acc. + infinitive structure arouses the expectation of some further structure that requires an infinitive, an expectation met with *quereris* (3): this is an indirect statement.

2   **nec quos praelegat** = *et quos non praelegat*; subjunctive of characteristic, the antecedent being *versus*

4   **coniugibus suis** dat. pl.; the function of the case becomes clear at the end of the next line (*placere* + dat.)

5   **mentula** This word was considered the obscenity *par excellence* (cf. 11.15) and thus comes with some emphasis here. Note the complacent masculinist assumption about what gives wives pleasure, and the interesting implications for the representation of the relationship between this poetry and its readers.

6   **quid si me iubeas . . .?** potential subjunctive: "What if you were to order me to . . .?" or "What if you were to tell me to . . .?"

7   **verbis . . . non thalassionis** gen. of characteristic, i.e., not with the characteristically coarse vocabulary of wedding songs

8   **quis Floralia vestit. . .?** The Floralia was an annual festival at Rome held in honor of the goddess Flora in late April and early May that included, among other things, performances of mimes at which actresses stripped off their clothes on stage. The question thus suggests a paradox, practically constitutes an oxymoron, and expects the answer: "No one!"

stolatum The *stola,* a garment that reached the feet, was the characteristic clothing of married Roman ladies (*matronae*), who were often represented as the antithesis of prostitutes (*meretrices*). Both halves of Martial's question rest on the assumption that public nudity and open enjoyment of sexuality have their place in Roman society just as much as do decent matrons.

10   **lex** as often, referring not to a piece of legislation but to a generally valid principle

11   **ne possint** a noun clause, in apposition to *lex*

pruriant Like the English derivative "prurient," the language of itching often has connotations of sexual stimulation in Latin. In a poem that almost certainly influenced Martial and that likewise uses the language of sexuality to talk about poetry, Catullus describes some of his poetry in terms of stimulation and itching (Catullus 16.9: *et quod pruriat incitare possunt*).

iuvare "give pleasure," repeating the idea of *placere* in 5

12   **quare** not the interrog. but the conj.: "therefore; and so . . ."

13   **parcas . . . rogamus** i.e., *rogamus ut parcas.* The use of the first person pl. to refer to oneself is widespread in literary Latin—even when, as here, it comes in close proximity to a first person sing. form (*meos*, 14)

14   **nec castrare velis** jussive subjunctive; equivalent to *et noli castrare*

15   **gallo . . . Priapo** an especially effective example of the line-framing technique, since the two names are diametrically opposed to each other. A *gallus* is a castrated priest of the mother-goddess Cybele (cf. 10.4, 14.204) and *Priapus* is the hypermasculine god of fertility renowned for one outstanding feature above all: his unusually large and frequently erect penis.

1.36

1   **Lucane . . . Tulle** As the poem quickly makes clear, they are
brothers. That is all we need to know in order to make sense of
this epigram, but elsewhere we learn more about them: their full
names were Cn. Domitius Lucanus and Cn. Domitius Tullus;
they were sons of Sextus Curvius and adopted by Domitius Afer;
they had the reputation of being devoted to each other; and they
pursued political careers in a more or less parallel fashion, each
becoming consul and subsequently proconsul of Africa. Martial
commemorates Lucanus' death in an epigram published about
94 CE in which he reverts to the themes of this poem (9.51), and
Pliny (*Epistulae* 8.18) narrates the sequel: bedridden and para-
lyzed, Tullus encouraged legacy-hunters (cf. 1.12.4) but left them
out of his will when he finally died around 107 CE.

tibi vel . . . tibi Note the scansion (*tibī . . . tibĭ*). This kind of
metrical play—repeating the same word within a single line using two different scansions—is not uncommon in Latin poetry,
particularly Ovid and Martial.

2   **qualia . . . habent** "the kind of destiny that the Spartan sons of
Leda have," referring to the mythic figures Castor and Pollux,
sons of Leda, wife of the Spartan king Tyndareus. Having mated
with Zeus, who had taken the form of a swan, Leda gave birth to
two daughters (Helen and Clytemnestra) and two sons (Castor
and Pollux). According to some stories, Castor was fully mortal
but Pollux half-divine; after Castor was killed in battle, Zeus
granted Pollux's request of sharing with his brother his privilege
of living amongst mortals and gods on alternate days, thus in
effect dividing his half-portion of divinity.

3   **haec** explained in the following line with the clause *quod . . . vel-
let uterque*

pietatis The virtue of *pietas,* most famously embodied by Vergil's Aeneas, entailed devotion to the gods, to one's country, and
to one's family members. In Rome's patriarchal society, the term
often suggested a man's devotion to his father, sons, or brothers.

4   A common theme in Latin epitaphs for children or spouses is that the survivor wishes he or she had died before, or instead of, the deceased.

5   The word order may be confusing: *et* is postponed, an implied *is* is understood as antecedent of *qui,* and the verb *diceret* constitutes a second apodosis of the conditional sentence whose protasis is *si darentur* (1): i.e., *et diceret (is) qui prior isset ad infernas umbras.*

    isset Note the tense of the subjunctive: this would occur prior to the action described by the verb *diceret.*

    umbras The word is frequently associated with the afterlife, sometimes referring to the shadowiness or gloominess of the underworld, sometimes to the spirits of the dead.

6   **vive ... meo** "live on your time, live on mine," i.e., use not only the time allotted to you but also that which has been destined for me. If given Pollux's choice, each brother would wish to die before the other and furthermore give up the half-share of life destined to him, so that his surviving brother might live even longer. Martial's verse seems to have inspired the composer of a poetic epitaph for a woman named Atilia Pomptilla in Cagliari (Sardinia), who predeceased her husband Philippus: *et prior at Lethen cum sit Pompti[ll]a recepta, / "tempore tu," dixit, "vive, Philippe, m[e]o"* (*Carmina Latina Epigraphica* 1551.3–4). Similarities and overlaps characterize Roman imagery for three important types of interpersonal relationship: between spouses, between brothers, and between male friends.

1.37

1   **ventris onus** a common euphemism for feces. These opening words underscore the jarring juxtaposition of this poem with the one before.

    misero ... auro i.e., a chamberpot made of gold—not even silver or bronze, let alone pottery! The adj., paradoxical if not oxymoronic when modifying this noun, ironically expresses sympathy for this valuable metal, being put to such a use.

2   Note how the pentameter falls into two distinct halves, each
     marked by a strong alliterative pattern (*b* in the first half, *c* in
     the second) and bluntly contrasting two bodily functions. The
     final word *cacas* restates the couplet's opening two words, shift-
     ing the tone from the euphemistic to the coarse.

1.47

1   The opening line of this punchy couplet is divided into two
     closely parallel halves at the caesura: an adv. of time beginning
     with *nu-* (*nuper, nunc*) is followed by a form of *esse* and a noun
     denoting a profession, and the line is capped off by the man's
     name. Experienced readers of Martial and of Latin literature in
     general will expect some kind of joke, since there was a long
     tradition of insulting doctors as charlatans or worse.

2   **quod** understand *id* as antecedent; the clause functions as the
     direct object of both verbs in this line. Note how the pentameter,
     too, falls neatly into two halves, but reversing the order of the
     first line, giving the couplet a chiastic stucture: *medicus - vispillo
     - vispillo - medicus*. Also worth noting is the juxtaposition of *facit*
     and *fecerat*, emphasizing the continuity in Diaulus' practice.

1.72

METER: Phalaecian hendecasyllable

1   **nostris versibus** abl. of cause; for the use of the first person pl.,
     cf. 1.35.13.

2   **Fidentine** To those who have read Book 1 straight through, this
     pseudonym will be familiar: three previous poems (1.29, 38, 53)
     have attacked Fidentinus for trying to pass off Martial's poetry
     as his own. In the absence of anything like copyright or other
     legal mechanisms for protecting authors' rights or prosecuting
     violations, and in a world in which poetry was not only bought,
     sold, and read in manuscripts (cf. 1.1–3) but orally recited in a
     variety of settings, the danger Martial describes was far from
     unrealistic.

3   **sic dentata sibi videtur** *sic* asserts a comparison ("in the same way . . ."); *dentata* is predicative and means "endowed with a beautiful set of teeth"; *sibi videtur,* as usual, means "thinks she is . . ." (lit., "seems to herself [to be] . . .")

4   False teeth were readily available to Romans who could afford them. They were often made of bone or ivory from the tusks of Indian elephants (*Indico cornu*).

5   **quae nigrior est** As often, the antecedent (*Lycoris*) comes after the rel. clause. Like Italian *nero* but unlike American English "black," the Latin adj. *niger,* when referring to human beings, does not necessarily suggest sub-Saharan African origins but more generally refers to dark features, hair, or complexion. As Martial's remark suggests, Roman women were often valued for being fair skinned or having light-colored hair; hence the cosmetic measures Lycoris takes.

    cadente i.e., fully ripe and thus ready to fall off the bush

6   **cerussata** *cerussa* was a white lead-based substance used as a basis for paint, medicines, and cosmetics. Women's makeup and hairstyling techniques are the subject of a number of Martial's epigrams as well as Ovid's poem *Medicamina faciei femineae.*

    sibi placet i.e., she likes the way she looks

7   **hac . . . ratione qua poeta es** "by the reasoning by which you are a poet," "in the same way you are a poet"

8   **calvus cum fueris, eris comatus** The line-framing adjs. underscore the paradox: Fidentinus will be bald, and yet have a head of hair (if we pursue the analogy to Aegle and Lycoris, he will be wearing a wig). Note the use of the fut. pf. to denote logical or temporal priority to the action described in the main clause.

1.93

1   **Fabricio . . . Aquinus** The line is framed by the two men's names, and the ABACB word order reflects how they are intertwined in the sleep of death. These men are mentioned nowhere else in Martial, but the epigram gives enough information to

make sense of the poem: they were close friends, both of them centurions who achieved the rank of *primus pilus*; Aquinus died before Fabricius, and they were eventually buried together in a tomb marked by epitaphs praising their loyal friendship. Hundreds of epitaphs surviving from the Roman world record the inclusion of friends within group burials along with spouses, relatives, and freedmen, and a handful commemorate the joint burial of two male or female friends alone.

Fig. 3. The Isola Sacra necropolis near Ostia: two adjacent burial enclosures with epitaphs above their entrances, and a separate altar-tomb for a child (epitaph not visible in photograph). Photograph by Craig Williams.

2   **prior Elysias . . . adisse domos** cf. 1.36, where the theme of rejoicing to have died before the other is applied to two brothers, and note the variation in the poetic language for death: in 1.36 *infernas ire ad umbras*, here *Elysias adire domos*.

3   **ara duplex** i.e., an altar-tomb for two people

primi testatur munera pili Epitaphs for Roman men of the upper classes typically cite any offices the deceased had held in life; the double tomb for Fabricius and Aquinus contains an inscription that publicizes the high military rank each had held. Coming with a significant pay increase, the title *primipilus* was given to the senior centurion of a legion. He held it for a year and afterwards was usually enrolled as a member of the equestrian order.

4   **plus** i.e., more significant

titulo quod breviore legis i.e., *id quod legis (in) breviore titulo.* The noun *titulus* denotes a text written on a label, placard, or stone or bronze surface, here referring to a second and shorter epitaph on the two men's tomb.

5   **iunctus uterque** Note the emphasis on the union of the two men, both in the repetition of *iunctus* from the first verse and in the adj. *uterque* ("each *of two*")

sacro . . . foedere The adj. can be translated "sacred" or "venerable," and the noun *foedus* refers to a variety of agreements, bonds, or compacts between states or individuals, especially spouses and friends. The etymologically related *fides* describes the basis of trust on which such connections were made (cf. 1.15.2). Cf. Catullus 109.6, usually understood to be describing Catullus' relationship with Lesbia: *aeternum hoc sanctae foedus amicitiae.*

6   **raro** adv.

amicus erat Note the emotive, idealizing language. It is hardly rare for two men to be friends; the point is that the friendship joining Aquinus and Fabricius was of an unusual and thus all the more praiseworthy intensity.

1.109

METER: Phalaecian hendecasyllable

1   **Issa** Note the striking repetition of the name at the beginning of the first five lines and the flattering comparatives in the first four (*nequior, purior, blandior, carior*). Not until the fifth repetition do we learn who Issa is. The name seems to be a popular pronunciation of *ipsa,* in the sense of *domina* (cf. Plautus *Casina* 790: *ego eo quo me ipsa misit*; Petronius *Satyricon* 63.3 *ipsimi nostri delicatus decessit*); an English parallel would be "Missy."

passere nequior Catulli The sparrow of Catullus 2 and 3 clearly had a reputation that lasted for generations; cf. 7.14. Like the English word "naughty," *nequam* can have an erotic connotation.

2   **osculo columbae** Doves—both female and male, notes Pliny the Elder with some surprise (*Naturalis Historia* 10.104)—were imagined in anthropomorphic terms to be "chaste" and "faithful" to their "spouses."

4   **Indicis lapillis** i.e., pearls

5   **deliciae catella** apposition ("pet dog"). The surprise that comes with *catella* is underscored by the fact that it breaks the sequence of compar. adjs. in lines 1–4. The noun *catellus, -a,* diminutive of *catulus, -a,* may refer either to a puppy or to a small dog of any age; an ancient epitaph found in the Veneto region of Italy commemorates a twelve-year-old *catellus* named Fuscus (*Année Épigraphique* 1994, no. 699).

6   **loqui** i.e., she speaks like a human being, the first of a series of details describing Issa as a dog who behaves remakably like a human. In a verse epitaph for a dog named Margarita ("Pearl") found in Rome we read: *et plus quam licuit muto canis ore loquebar* (*Corpus Inscriptionum Latinarum* 6.29896.9).

7   To many it goes without saying that dogs experience sadness and joy, but the fact that Martial makes the point suggests that some of his readership would find it less than obvious. Alternatively, the phrase *tristitiamque gaudiumque* refers to *Publius'* sadness and happiness, which Issa is said to perceive, but the preceding line seems to suggest an emphasis on Issa's humanlike characteristics.

8   **collo nixa** "resting on his (Publius') neck." A verse epitaph for a dog found near Salerno in southern Italy includes the lines: *ergo mihi, Patrice, iam non dabis oscula mille / nec poteris collo grata cubare meo* (*Corpus Inscriptionum Latinarum* 10.659.3–4).

     capitque somnos Phrases like *somnum capere* or *quietem capere* mean "to rest, to take a nap."

9   **ut ... sentiantur** result clause, although there is no marker such as *ita* or *tam* in the main clause

10   **desiderio . . . ventris** see on 1.37.1; as the next line shows, the euphemism here refers to urination rather than defecation

11   **pallia non fefellit** i.e., she has never made a mess on the sheets. This use of *fallere* ("deceive, trick") is unparalleled in extant Latin, but may be related to expressions like *fidem fallere* or *conubia fallere,* where the verb is similar in meaning to *violare.* The idea may be that, if Issa were to urinate on the sheets, she would be violating both an implicit agreement with Publius and the sheets themselves.

12   **suscitat** understand Publius as the direct object.

   toroque abl. of separation ("from the couch")

13   **levari** either "to be picked back up" (after she has done what she needed to do) or "to be given relief" (compare the English euphemism "to relieve oneself"). The former yields a line whose chiastic structure is reflected in its sense as well, *deponi* and *levari* being complementary in meaning.

15   **ignorat** We might have expected a result clause (*tantus . . . ut ignoret*), but a paratactic structure such as this was also possible and apparently colloquial. Cf. English "I'm so hungry, I could eat a cow" for "I'm so hungry that I could eat a cow."

   Venerem The name of the goddess and phrases like *res veneriae* are used by Latin writers to refer to the realm of the sexual. Issa has taken the feminine virtues of *castitas* and *pudor* to the extreme of having no sexual experience at all.

   invenimus The meter makes the tense of the verb clear (this is an ongoing search), and the pl. implies that Martial and Publius—and perhaps others too—are working together on the question of finding a husband for Issa.

16   **virum puella** With these significantly juxtaposed words the process of anthropomorphizing Issa is complete.

17   **lux . . . suprema** i.e., the day of her death. The adj. *supremus* ("final, ultimate") is not infrequently associated with death

18   **picta . . . tabella** "on a painted tablet" i.e., Publius has painted a portrait of Issa, or else (more likely) commissioned one

20   The thought is paradoxical to the point of being dizzying, but
     the syntax is clear: *ut sit* is a result clause motivated by *tam simi-*
     lem in the preceding line; the subject of *sit* is *nec ipsa* (punning
     on the name *Issa*); the predicate is *tam similis sibi*, a phrase that
     lies at the heart both of the line and of the paradox: "so that not
     even she herself is as similar to herself [as the portrait is]." The
     extreme realism of works of visual art is a common theme in
     Greek and Latin epigram.

21   **denique** as often, not marking the last of a series ("finally") but
     wrapping things up: "So then . . ." or "In short . . ."

     pone cum i.e., put her next to her portrait

1.110

1   **Velox** Mr. Swift complains that Martial's epigrams take too long
     to read. Some of Martial's pseudonyms are clearly not random,
     and the German phrase *redende Namen*, "speaking names," is
     sometimes used to describe the technique. Velox's complaint
     was by no means idiosyncratic, since the genre of epigram came
     with an expectation of concision and brevity (see Introduction);
     thus the phrase *epigrammata longa* is practically oxymoronic.
     Furthermore, the juxtaposition of this two-line epigram with
     the preceding twenty-three–line poem on Issa calls attention to
     itself (see 1.34 and 1.35 for another example of paired epigrams)
     and makes the point that Martial is capable of writing epigrams
     of varying lengths.

2   **breviora** understand *epigrammata*. The technique of reporting
     criticism of his own poetry and responding to it with a witty or
     ironic attack on his critics is characteristic of Martial.

1.118

1   **cui . . . satis non est** understand *is* as antecedent of the rel. pron.;
     "whoever is not satisifed with . . ."

     epigrammata centum Roughly one hundred epigrams per
     book seems to be Martial's ideal. The shortest book (8) contains

eighty-two and, as it happens, Book 1 is the longest: this, the 118th epigram, is the book's last.

2   **illi** referring back to the indef. subject of the preceding line

mali partitive gen. with *satis*. The epigram, and with it the book, ends on a note of self-criticism, albeit qualified. Martial is not describing *all* of his poetry as "bad" (cf. 1.16), but making the point that if the collection becomes too long it will cause his readers to suffer, and that anyone who actually likes reading a collection of more than one hundred epigrams is a literary masochist.

∾ *Book 2*

2.5

1   **ne valeam** lit. "may I not be well," i.e., may I become ill if what I say is not true. This and similar expressions (such as the even stronger *dispeream si . . .* or *ne vivam si . . .*) were an apparently colloquial way of forcefully backing up an assertion (cf. the different metaphor in the English expression "[I'll be] damned if . . .").

Deciane Martial addresses the prose preface to Book 2 to Decianus (for whom, see 1.24.1); that he includes this teasing epigram in the same book is emblematic of his lightly ironic touch. Decianus never appears again after Book 2, and there have been various speculations as to why: did he die, was he disgraced, did he and Martial have a falling out?

totis . . . diebus / et . . . totis noctibus The polar expression, an emphatic way of communicating the idea "always," is typical of the enthusiastic assertions frequently found in the language of Roman friendship, and is hardly expressing a desire to literally spend twenty-four hours a day with Decianus.

3   **duo** take with *milia passum*

quae nos disiungunt i.e., which lie between my home and yours; the antecedent of the rel. pron. is *milia*. Instead of *disiungunt,* found in the sole manuscript representing family α, families β and γ read *distinguunt*, which is little different in meaning. Either reading could be correct, and modern editors are not unanimous.

milia passum the pl. of *mille passus*, "a thousand paces, a mile." *Passum,* partitive gen., is an alternative to *passuum*; a few other 4th-declension nouns have the same alternative gen. pl. (e.g., *currum, manum, exercitum*). A Roman mile is equivalent to about 4,855 feet and thus somewhat shorter than the modern mile.

5   **negaris** understand *esse domi*. Decianus' slaves announce to visitors that their master is not home even though he is (sometimes obviously so)—a situation not unheard of in many urban societies, and the subject of jokes and complaints elsewhere in Latin literature.

7   **non piget** understand *me*: "I don't mind"

8   **quattuor ire piget** A subtle but perceptible threat: Martial may sooner or later stop going to the effort of making the trip if it continues to be pointless. Note how this poem has progressed from the strong enthusiasm of the opening couplet to the strong reservations of this final couplet. Complaints that efforts at maintaining a friendship are unrequited or feebly reciprocated are a common theme in Martial's poetry.

2.11

Meter: Scazon

1   **Selium** Martial uses this name in three other poems of Book 2 to refer to a man who shows the same obsession revealed at the end of this poem.

fronte . . . nubila abl. of characteristic; the adj. suggests gloomy preoccupation

Rufe a common cognomen and, after Caesar (126 occurrences), the most frequently occurring of all personal names in Martial's poetry (33 occurrences, closely followed by Flaccus with 31). Sometimes reference to a specific man is hinted at by means of a *nomen gentilicium,* but not in this poem, where the name is more than anything else a device to create an atmosphere of lively discussion.

2   **ambulator porticum terit seram** It was a common habit among Romans of Martial's day to take strolls through the porticoes of the Campus Martius in the late afternoon and early evening. As this poem suggests, these outings might sometimes have a specific goal.

3   **quod tacet** Note the marked postponement of the conj. *quod*, in contrast to lines 1–2 and 4–5. The phrase *lugubre quiddam . . . tacet* means that Selius' facial expression hints at some unspoken grief.

    piger vultus repeating but varying the idea of *fronte nubila* in line 1. The adj. is unusual as a descriptor of a facial expression, but seems to suggest sluggish sadness.

4   **indecens** The adj. is either attributive with *nasus* ("ugly nose")— making fun of people's physical appearance was a standard and fully acceptable technique of Roman humor—or else predicative with *tangit* ("indecently touches the ground"), a criticism of Selius' exaggerated behavior.

5   **dextra** The meter does not reveal whether this is nom. sing. or abl. sing., but the parallel with *vellit* in the same line invites us to understand Selius as the subject of *pulsat* as well, and thus *dextra* as abl. Both actions—beating the breast and tearing at one's hair—were traditional gestures expressing extreme grief, usually (as the next lines suggest) at someone's death.

6   **amici . . . aut fratris** The first two possible explanations for Selius' distress are not randomly chosen: in Rome's masculine culture, friendship between men and brotherly love were among the most highly valued of relationships.

    fata Throughout Greek and Latin literature, the concept of a human being's "fate" or "destiny" is closely linked to his or her death in particular rather than to the vicissitudes of life in general.

7   **vivit et precor vivat** i.e., *vivit et precor (ut) vivat (diu)*. The syntax, with repetition of the verb in indicative and then subjunctive, expresses a fervent (here ironic) wish. In Ovid we find phrases like *pervenit perveniatque precor* or *facis faciasque precor*.

8   **uxor sarcinaeque servique** A passing reminder of the social class
     to which Martial belonged, for which he wrote, and whose mem-
     bers are the protagonists of his poetry: free men with enough
     resources to own slaves. Not necessarily extremely wealthy, since
     even Romans of modest means could afford one or two cheap
     slaves, they were not desperately poor either.

9   **colonus vilicusque** This gives further specificity to Selius' so-
     cial status: he owns a country estate that is managed by a *vilicus*
     (a slave who had the job of overseeing the estate including the
     other slaves) and farmed by a *colonus*.

     decoxit lit., "boiled down, melted away"; used metaphorically to
     describe the squandering of money or resources

10   **maeroris** This noun and the related adj. *maestus* usually refer to
     an intense grief, often at someone's death.

     causa quae the interrog., not the rel.; understand *est*. Posing a
     question and then supplying its answer is one of Martial's favor-
     ite techniques for bringing an epigram to its climactic ending.

     domi cenat Why does Selius show such extravagant gestures of
     distress? The answer comes with the poem's two final words—
     and is quite a surprise. Other epigrams on Selius in Book 2 ex-
     pand upon this picture of a man desperate for dinner invita-
     tions. While Martial is mocking him as an extreme case, dining
     alone at home could indeed be taken as a sign of social isolation
     or rejection in the group-oriented world of Martial's Rome.

2.18

1   **capto** In the first occurrence of the word in this line the final
     -o counts as short (cf. 1.24.4), but in the second as long; for
     the technique, cf. 1.36.1. Note how this line builds up to and is
     framed by a wry confession: it is not clear what *tuam* refers to,
     and therefore what Martial is chasing after, until the final word
     (*cenam*, i.e., dinner at Maximus' home) and the repetition of
     capto with interjected *pudet heu* adds to the ironically pathetic

tone. The speaker of this poem is no Selius, but it is worth noting that he casts himself in the role of one who hunts for dinner invitations.

Maxime a common cognomen. We cannot know whether Martial addressed this poem to any one man in particular and, if so, which one.

2   **aliam** i.e., *alienam* ("dinner at someone else's house"), parallel to *tuam cenam* in the preceding line

3   **salutatum** supine; here, as often in Martial, this verb refers to the *salutatio* or morning reception at which Romans in the role of client went to their patrons' homes in order to pay their respects and, with luck, receive something in return, such as food or cash.

4   **ante** not the prep. but the adv., equivalent to *antea*

5   In addition to participating in the *salutatio,* Roman clients might accompany their patron in public, leading him down a street or forming a crowd around him in a display of his power and influence. Like the opening line, the second half of this verse seems self-disparaging: *tumidi . . . regis* suggests an arrogant patron (the noun *rex* was an honorific way of referring to a patron, but came with a powerful ambivalence: cf. spect.2.3), and the noun *anteambulo* can refer to a slave who walked in front of his master on the street, corresponding to the *pedisequi* behind him.

6   **iam sumus ergo pares** Now that this phrase has been repeated for the third time at the end of each couplet, a pattern has clearly been established. When it is broken in the next and final couplet, all the more emphasis is placed on what is said there.

7   **vicarius** a slave who served another slave. This is not the only epigram in which Martial uses the language of slavery to describe the bond between patron and client, seen from the latter's perspective. It is hard to know how serious the social criticism is, but in any case the rhetorical self-indulgence was characteristic of those who were not actually slaves.

8   **Maxime** For the repetition of the vocative from the first line, cf.
     1.34.10.

     non habeat The use of *non* instead of *ne* with both jussive and
     optative subjunctives is not uncommon in Latin poetic texts of
     all periods as well as in later prose.

2.19

1   **Zoile** Like Selius (cf. 2.11) and Postumus (cf. 2.21), Zoilus is a
     recurring figure in Book 2; he appears in other books as well.
     There appears to be some degree of continuity in epigrams us-
     ing the name Zoilus: he is a former runaway slave (*fugitivus*)
     who had obtained his freedom, and his traits include flaunting
     his wealth while being a stingy host, as well as a propensity for
     oral sex. The name recalls a fourth-century BCE Cynic philoso-
     pher known for his sharp attacks on Homer and Plato; note its
     insistent triple occurrence in this epigram.

     cena abl. of cause; the theme of dinner parties continues from
     the previous poem

2   The pointed repetition of *felicem* is intensified by *deinde* and the
     addition of *tua*: not just any dinner, but *your* dinner, of all things?

3   **Aricino ... clivo** A slope on the Appian Way about sixteen miles
     from Rome near the town of Aricia was well known as a place
     where beggars gathered, presumably because vehicles traveling
     the road had to slow down considerably at this point. In other
     words, Zoilus' dinners would satisfy only beggars.

     conviva recumbere the noun is predicative ("recline as a din-
     ner-guest"). At formal dinners Roman men generally did not sit
     on chairs but reclined (*recumbere, accumbere*) on couches posi-
     tioned next to low tables (*mensae*) containing food and drink.
     Here the verb plays with the idea that the beggars near Aricia are
     reclining not on a couch in a comfortable dining room, but on a
     slope beside a heavily travelled road.

4   With this, the third occurrence of the phrase *felicem cena*, a live-
     ly variation on the technique of tricolon crescendo is effected.

2.20

1   **carmina . . . emit** For the commercial aspects of poetry in Martial's Rome, cf. 1.2, 1.3.

recitat Recitations of poetry in various public and semi-public settings were common, from gatherings in theaters and basilicas to private dinner-parties. Juvenal's first satire opens with an expression of frustration at being subjected to countless recitations of bad poetry, even in the hot summer months.

2   **quod emas** rel. clause of characteristic, antecedent *id* understood

possis potential subjunctive

iure the abl. sing. of *ius*, used adverbially and modifying *possis*. Both its broader meaning ("rightly, properly") and the narrower legal sense ("in accordance with the laws") are relevant.

2.21

1   Note the chiastic structure (*das aliis, aliis das*) with its juxtaposition of the repeated *aliis* in a line that is framed by the two direct objects of the repeated verb *das*.

Postume a name used by Martial in Books 1–6 to describe a variety of characters, most of them unpleasant. This epigram forms part of a so-called "cycle" within Book 2 on the subject of a man whose kisses are repulsive (2.10, 2.12, 2.21–23).

2   **malo manum** a pithy retort whose effect is heightened by the alliteration; *manum* repeats with variation the idea of *dextram* at the end of the preceding line. Since it was normal Roman practice for men to greet friends and acquaintances with a kiss, why is Martial so eager to avoid Postumus' kisses? For experienced readers of Latin literature the obvious possibilities include bad breath and/or an inclination for performing oral sex.

2.22

1   **quid mihi vobiscum est** "Why do I have anything to do with
     you?" or "Why do I bother with you?"

     o Phoebe novemque sorores Phoebus is Apollo and "the nine
     sisters" are the Muses, goddesses of artistic creativity and inspi-
     ration. The vocative particle *o* and the periphrasis for the Muses
     give the line a lofty tone, and the entire first couplet seems to be
     inspired by Ovid's exile poetry, in which he meditates upon the
     damage that his earlier poetry had done him (cf. *Tristia* 2.1: *quid
     mihi vobiscum est, infelix cura, libelli?*; 3.2.5: *Musa iocosa mea*;
     3.14.6: *artifici quae nocuere suo*). This makes the revelation in
     the next couplet that much more humorously jarring.

2   **vati** From the Augustan period onwards, this noun ("prophet,
     fortune-teller") was used as an elevated and respectful term for
     poets ("bard")—often, as here, in self-referential poetry.

3   **dimidio** Only in the following clause do we learn what this
     adj. modifies (*labro*), an example of the structure known as
     apo koinou ("from a shared element"), in which two clauses or
     phrases share a key element found in only one of them. As the
     contrast with *utroque* in line 4 shows, the unusual phrase *di-
     midio labro* means not "with half a lip" but "with half his lips."

     ante adv., i.e., *antea*; referring not just to some imaginary prior
     time but quite concretely to an earlier poem (2.10.1–2: *basia di-
     midio quod das mihi, Postume, labro, / laudo*). Internal cross-
     referencing of this kind is typical of the sophisticated play char-
     acteristic of Latin poetry.

4   **basia** Emphatically placed at the beginning of the poem's final
     verse, this word fills out the picture and shifts the tone from
     the loftily serious to the wryly humorous. Far from Ovid's ban-
     ishment to far-off Tomis, Martial's fame as a poet has brought
     him—Postumus' nasty kisses.

2.23

METER: Phalaecian hendecasyllable

1 **licet . . . rogetis** As often, this construction expresses concession: "granted that you ask," hence, "though you may ask." Once again Martial addresses his anonymous readership, this time (contrast 1.1) in the pl.

2 **qui sit Postumus** indirect question. His readers' desire to know who the "real" Postumus is implies that they assume that there is indeed a real man behind the name. Here too Martial follows in the footsteps of Ovid (*Ars Amatoria* 3.538: *et multi, quae sit nostra Corinna, rogant*; cf. *Tristia* 4.10.60: *nomine non vero dicta Corinna mihi*). It has, however, plausibly been suggested that no one person actually lay behind pseudonyms like Corinna or Postumus, and that by means of poems like this, poets playfully induced the assumption that there was.

4 **has offendere basiationes** a compressed expression: it is not literally the kisses that Martial would offend by revealing Postumus' identity, but Postumus himself. As opposed to the common *basium,* the abstraction *basiatio* is attested only in Catullus and Martial and probably humorously elevated in tone.

5 **se . . . vindicare** i.e., Postumus would take revenge for the revelation of his identity by planting more kisses on Martial's mouth.

2.26

1 **querulum** n. acc. sing. of the adj. used adverbially; similarly *acerbum*. The first adj. suggests a combination of wheezing and lamenting, the second a hacking cough.

tussit cf. 1.10.4, where this very word constitutes the sharp point of the epigram. Experienced readers of Martial may already suspect that something is up with Naevia's cough.

2 **mittit sputa** a probably humorous periphrasis for *sputat* or *spuit*. Since *mitto* often takes objects like *telum* or *hastam*, the imagery is fairly drastic: Naevia is discharging or letting her spit fly as if it were a weapon.

sinus a word with a wide range of meanings, particularly evocative here: "the folds of your toga," "your lap," or "your bosom." Since *sinus* often occurs in erotically charged contexts, there may be a hint that Naevia and the addressee are lovers. In any case the combination of nouns in the half-line *sputa subinde sinus* is grotesque, the effect heightened by the alliterations.

3   **te rem factam . . . credis habere?** *rem factam habere* is an idiomatic expression ("you think you've got it made?"). The question-and-answer format marks the climax of the epigram; cf. 2.17.10.

4   **erras** The positioning and isolation of this word give it that much more emphasis.

    blanditur In other words, she is manipulating her *captator* (cf. 1.10) to her own advantage. Like *sinus* above, this verb often occurs in erotically charged scenes and is thus strongly paradoxical here: this is how Naevia flirts with Bithynicus!

2.28

1   **multum** adverbial with *rideto*

    qui understand *eum* as antecedent

    Sextille The name occurs only here in Martial's epigrams.

    cinaedum an untranslatable insult. Denoting an effeminate dancer, it can also be used non-literally as an insult, describing a man as effeminate and inclined (though not exclusively) to playing the receptive role in anal intercourse.

2   **dixerit** fut. pf. indicative, logically prior to the time of the fut. imperative *rideto*: if someone will have called you a *cinaedus*, you can (then) laugh at him.

    digitum . . . medium the aggressive and still common gesture, sometimes called by Romans *digitus impudicus* or *digitus infamis*. Its phallic symbolism is particularly appropriate here: Sextillus can refute the accusation of being a *cinaedus* by means of this gestural assertion of penetrative masculinity.

3   **sed nec pedico es** This begins a description of three sexual roles that a Roman man might play without damage to his masculine image: *pedico* (alternatively *pedicator*) is an obscene noun referring to a man who anally penetrates his partners, whether male or female; *fututor* is the corresponding obscenity referring to a man who vaginally penetrates his female partners; line 4 is a periphrasis for the noun *irrumator,* referring to a man who orally penetrates his male or female partners. While Sextillus can refute the accusation of being an effeminate *cinaedus,* Martial now observes that he plays none of the acceptably masculine penetrative roles either. This builds up to the puzzled question and insinuating response at the epigram's end.

4   **Vetustinae** a name found only here in Martial's poetry. Perhaps, like *Vetustilla* in 3.93, it suggests an aging prostitute. Horace, *Epodes* 8, plays with the notion that an unattractive older woman might only be able to stimulate her male partner by means of fellatio.

    nec postponed; i.e., *nec tibi placet calda Vetustinae bucca*

6   **nescio, sed tu scis** The near juxtaposition of the contrasting verbs builds up to the final blow, as feigned ignorance is combined with the smug remark that Sextillus knows the answer.

    res superesse duas "that two things (i.e., possibilities) remain." The Roman linguistic and conceptual system for categorizing men as sexual agents makes it clear that the two remaining options are *fellator* and *cunnilingus*: the insinuation is that Sextillus performs oral sex on either male or female partners. A number of Latin texts represent these two roles as the most degrading of all for a man, even more than that of the effeminate *cinaedus* invoked in line 1. In the end, this epigram makes a sharp jab at Sextillus even as it adopts a tone of friendly (mock-) innocence.

2.30

1   **viginti sestertia** When referring to large amounts of sesterces,
    Latin writers often elide the word *milia*. Twenty thousand ses-
    terces is a solid amount of money, but not astronomical: Mar-
    tial describes the same amount as a high price to pay for a deaf
    slave (11.38) and in another epigram refers to a loan of 100,000
    sesterces (6.20).

    forte adv., "by chance, as it happened"; related to *fors, fortasse,* and
    fortuna, and not to be confused with the adj. *fortis, -e* ("strong").
    Together with the tense of the verb *rogabam,* this creates a tone of
    vivid storytelling ("I happened to be asking for a loan, when . . .")

    rogabam Martial often, as here, writes in the persona of some-
    one requesting a loan; in one poem (6.10) he even asks the em-
    peror! Sometimes, however, he speaks in the voice of one who
    has been asked for, or has already given, a loan.

2   **quae . . . munus erat** As usual, the rel. pron. agrees in gender
    and number with its antecedent (n. pl. *sestertia*); the verb *erat*
    agrees in number with its predicate nom. (n. sing. *munus*).

    vel donanti "even if he were to give it to me outright" (rather
    than as a loan)

3   **fidusque vetusque sodalis** A proverb expressed in a range of
    Greek and Latin texts holds that "friends share everything." Mar-
    tial here brings out one implication of this ideal in a forthright
    manner not atypical of Roman culture: if your friends have more
    resources than you do, you should be able to count on their sup-
    port when you need it. The adj. *fidus* is found in the manuscripts
    of family β, whereas families α and γ read *felix* ("rich"), which is
    what Lindsay prints in his Oxford Classical Texts edition. Both
    adjs. make sense here, but *fidus* is a key item in the traditional
    vocabulary of Roman friendship (cf. 1.15.2), and *felix* seems awk-
    wardly redundant in combination with the following line.

4   **laxas arca flagellat opes** The adj. ("loose, roomy, spacious") here
    apparently means "ample"; its use to refer to money is unusual,
    and the metaphor—"his cash-box whips his ample riches"—is

vivid but not entirely clear. One explanation is that the money is not allowed to stay put in the cash-box but is always kept on the move (e.g., by being lent out at interest) in order to get the greatest return. Another possibility is that, on the contrary, the money is being disciplined, i.e., hoarded and thus prevented from leaving the cash-box.

5 **si causas egeris** The phrase *causas agere* refers to pleading cases in the courtroom. Martial frequently draws a contrast between a remunerative career in law and the relative poverty attending his life as a poet; but see 8.17.

6 **Gai** The name *Gaius* was so common that it could be used to denote "any chance person, like Tom, Dick, and Harry" (*Oxford Latin Dictionary* s.v. c). Note the shift from third-person narrative in lines 1–5 to a second-person address in the final verse, a characteristic technique that often signals the two halves of a bipartite epigram: cf. 1.33.3.

non peto consilium The concluding joke is driven home by the repetition of *peto* within the line, located in the same metrical position in each hemistich (half-line). Note how it varies the near-synonym *rogabam* in the poem's opening line—a verb whose object reminds us of what Martial *is* asking for.

2.37

METER: Phalaecian hendecasyllable

1 **ponitur** i.e., is put before you on the table

2 **mammas suminis** sow's udder, a delicacy, the first in a rapid, impressive accumulation of dishes

3 **communem duobus** i.e., big enough for two

4 **dimidium . . . totum** note the balanced contrast

5–6 Note the chiastic order of each line and the juxtaposition of different parts of two animals in line 5.

7 **madente** i.e., dripping with the oils and juices of all the food that has been stuffed into it

8   **puero** It was customary for Romans who had slaves to bring one
     or more along with them when they went out on social calls or
     to dinner parties.

9   **nos accumbimus** The shift of focus from *your* behavior to *our*
     reaction (or lack of it) is sudden and effective, signaled by the
     emphatic pron. at the beginning of the line. For the meaning of
     the verb, cf. 2.19.3.

     otiosa turba in apposition to *nos*; the parallelism of pl. and sing.
     is perfectly normal, since the noun *turba* (also describing the
     guests at a banquet at 1.20.1) refers to a group. The adj. suggests
     that the dinner-guests have nothing more to do since Caecilia-
     nus has been so efficient, and/or that they are powerless to react.

10   **ullus si pudor est** understand *tibi,* dat. of possession. Expres-
     sions like this ("if you have any sense of decency") are found in
     a range of Latin as a means of shaming someone into action.

11   **Caeciliane** The badly behaved guest's name (cf. 1.20.2) is finally
     revealed—a fairly unusual postponement of the vocative.

     vocavi As often, the verb *vocare* here means "invite to dinner."
     With this, the epigram's final word, not only is a witty paradox
     established by the line-framing *cras . . . non vocavi*, but we learn
     that Martial is imagining himself in the role of host (as opposed
     to 2.19 and a number of other epigrams in which he speaks
     in the voice of a dinner-guest). In a gesture that is as rhetori-
     cally effective as it is polite, he has identified himself with the
     other dinner-guests (*nos*), and the epigram also acquires a self-
     advertising function: he can put on an impressive dinner.

2.44

Meter: Phalaecian hendecasyllable

1   **emi seu puerum togamve** In English the conj. comes before the
     verb: "whether I have bought a slave-boy or a toga . . . "

     pexam Since togas were made of wool and with time and/or
     improper care could become nappy, "freshly combed" suggests
     "brand-new."

2   **ut puta** an idiomatic expression roughly equivalent to English "say" or "for example"

   libras understand *argenti*

3   **fenerator** In the absence of banks in the modern sense, Romans wishing to borrow money would either ask friends or relatives for loans (cf. 2.33) or go to men called *feneratores*, who made a living by lending money at usually exorbitant interest rates (*fenus* = "interest"). The peculiarity of the situation imagined in this poem, and the sharpness of the point, lies in the fact that the *fenerator* Sextus also happens to be an "old pal" of the speaker's (*veterem meum sodalem*, 4)—unless the phrase is an ironic way of signaling that he and Sextus have a long-standing professional relationship.

5   **ne ... petam** dependent upon both *timet* and *cavet*, thus simultaneously functioning as a fear clause and an object clause

6   **secum ... susurrat** Note that while the English idiom is "to talk *to* oneself," in Latin (as in Italian) one talks *with* oneself.

   ut audiam either a purpose clause or a result clause (i.e., *ita ut audiam*); sometimes the distinction is hard to make

7   **septem milia** understand gen. pl. *sestertium*. As happens in many languages, when the context precludes any misunderstanding, Latin speakers might omit the unit of currency when naming an amount of money.

8   Note the arrangement of the words and the alliterative pattern of the two names.

9   **quadrans** Having the value of one-fourth of an *as,* the *quadrans* was the smallest denomination of coin circulating in Martial's day, thus as a metaphor equivalent to English "penny." Since in Martial's day one *as* was in turn one-fourth of a sesterce, this stands in drastic contrast with the total of 22,000 sesterces Sextus claims to owe to others.

11-12 Note the shift from third-person narrative (*Sextus ... susurrat*) to lively second-person address (*durum est, Sexte*); cf. 1.33.3. There is also a contrast between the indicative *cum rogaris* (when someone actually asks you for a loan) and the subjunctive *antequam rogeris* (even before someone gets around to asking you).

2.62

1 **quod pectus** the first of three body parts named in this line, all governed by the verb that comes at the end. The conj. *quod* introduces a noun clause: "(the fact) that you pluck the hair from . . ."

tibi dat. of reference, equivalent in effect to a possessive adj.

2 **pilis** abl. pl. of *pilus, -i*; i.e., he has neatly trimmed his pubic hair

3 **hoc** i.e., everything that has just been described in the preceding *quod*-clauses

amicae dat. of advantage ("for the sake of . . ."). In the language of Latin literary texts (but not of epitaphs and other inscriptions), to refer to a man's *amica* is to signify that she is his sexual partner or "girlfriend." A number of Latin texts describe men who, in order to make themselves sexually attractive to women, depilate various parts of their bodies, and Martial's detailed list gives a not atypical overview of which parts. When taken too far, such care of the body could be described as effeminate; note that in Roman terms effeminacy has no necessary connection with homosexuality.

4 **praestas** the direct object consists of the *quod*-clause that follows

culum This word, strictly referring to the anus rather than the buttocks (though, as with its derivatives in the Romance languages, the distinction is not always maintained), communicates the essence of the joke. The implication is that in addition to his girlfriend, Labienus has a male sexual partner who anally penetrates him. Erotic constellations of this kind are described in other Latin texts as well. The slur being made against Labienus is not that he has a male partner, but that he plays the receptive or "passive" role in intercourse with him.

pilas from the verb *pilo, -are,* denoting the removal of bodily hair by various means, including plucking (*vellere,* as in line 1), waxing, singeing or rubbing with pumice, as opposed to shaving with a razor (*radere*) or trimming with scissors (*tondere*).

2.80

1   **hostem cum fugeret** Since the noun *hostis* usually signifies a military opponent (as opposed to *inimicus*, which can refer to any kind of personal enemy), Fannius apparently killed himself in order to avoid falling into enemy hands.

  Fannius Suetonius and Dio tell of a Fannius Caepio who was condemned to death in 22 BCE, but Dio in particular implies that he was killed by others. If Martial is indeed referring to a historical figure, this was almost certainly another man named Fannius, but the entire scenario may be invented.

2   **non furor est** Note the stance of incomprehension at Fannius' suicide, underscored by the paradox in the second half of the line and given further urgency by the parenthetical *rogo*, as if the speaker were engaging in a heated conversation. In fact, attitudes toward suicide among Romans varied widely. Many (including most Stoics) saw it as an acceptable and sometimes even laudable way out of certain intolerable situations, such as incurable physical suffering or an imminent and disgraceful death at someone else's hand. Some famous suicides, such as that of Cato the Younger, were models of Roman dignity, and Martial himself elsewhere praises brave acts of suicide (cf. 1.13).

  ne moriare, mori The paradox is explored in a number of philosophical texts, but Martial's formulation is perhaps specifically inspired by Seneca, *Epistles* 70.8: *stultitia est timore mortis mori*. Note how Martial's extremely compressed phrasing intensifies the effect.

2.82

1 **figis** apparently implying *cruci*, although the verb *figo* alone usually refers to stabbing. A number of Roman writers—including Seneca, Martial himself, and Juvenal—describe and condemn the mistreatment of slaves; for the brutal combination mentioned here, cf. Cicero *pro Cluentio* 187.

2 **populum** more emphatic than, for example, *multos*: the entire citizen body is talking about this

quod tacet ille understand *id* as antecedent; the clause is the direct object of *loqui*. Martial's criticism is aimed not so much at the cruelty of Ponticus' deed as its futility, and the epigram reads like a piece of gossip, stirring up (without satisfying) curiosity as to the nature of Ponticus' secret. The name appears in several books of Martial; as usual, it is debatable whether a single character is at stake.

∾ *Book 3*

3.1

1 **hoc** i.e., *hunc librum*; a reminder of the historical origins of the genre of epigram as text inscribed on an object

tibi The pron. raises the question of whether a specific addressee will be named; by the time we finish the poem we realize there is none. For Martial's appeals to his anonymous readers, cf. 1.1.4.

2 **Gallia** The term referred both to *Gallia Transalpina* (roughly modern France and also known as *Gallia Comata* because its inhabitants traditionally wore their hair long) and to the part of the Italian peninsula north of the Padanus (Po), called *Gallia Cisalpina* ("on this side of the Alps") or *Gallia Togata* (hence *Romanae . . . togae*) because its inhabitants generally adopted Roman dress, the Latin language, and other signs of Roman culture. Book 3 of Martial's epigrams was sent to Rome in 87 CE from the town of Forum Cornelii, today Imola, in Gallia Cisalpina (cf. 3.4).

3 **librum . . . priorem** i.e., Book 2. Martial's epigrams periodically make reference to their organization in numbered books; cf. 6.1.

4 **illa vel haec** i.e., both the previous book and this one. Latin often uses the n. pl. of demonstratives (*haec* and *illa*) where English uses the sing. ("this" and "that").

quae meliora putas "whichever [book] you consider to be better." Note the flattery of the reader, the stance of dependence on his or her judgment.

5 **sane** concessive ("and yet . . .")

domina . . . in urbe cf. 1.3.3

6 **Gallum** in the sense "from Gallia," but possibly with a play on the noun *gallus*, -*i*, referring to a castrated priest of Cybele (cf. 1.35.15). The noun *verna*, here in apposition to *liber*, denotes a slave who was born in the owner's home as opposed to one who was bought at a market or captured in war. Note the contrast with *domina*, and cf. 1.3 for the technique of personifying the book as well as the metaphor of book as slave. The final line combines ethnocentric sentiment with a complacent comparison between urban and provincial life to the detriment of the latter.

3.27

1 For the meaning of *vocare* cf. 2.37.11; *revocare* refers to returning the favor with an invitation of one's own. Note the contrasts around which the line is built: *numquam* vs. *saepe*, *revocas* vs. *vocatus*.

2 **si modo** "but only if . . ."

Galle The name occurs frequently in Martial's epigrams, attached to a wide variety of characters.

3 **invitas alios** Note the adversative asyndeton, an abrupt contrast emphasized by the lack of connective (cf. 1.33.2); in a translation we might supply "but" or "yet."

utriusque understand *nostrum* (as becomes clear in the next line)

4 **mihi cor non est** With connotations unlike those of English "heart" and closer to those of "brain," Latin *cor* suggests intelligence and perception.

pudor the sense of shame that is often invoked in Latin texts as a principle on which proper behavior rests; it is related to fear of what others might say and to concern for one's reputation. The point might be paraphrased: I'm brainless and you're shameless. The fairly strong language helps contextualize Martial's recurring allusions to proper behavior in connection with dinner parties. These are questions not just of etiquette or niceties, but of deeply important principles of social behavior.

3.43

1 **mentiris iuvenem** understand *te esse*, a common usage with *mentiri*, which in this sense is similar in meaning to *simulare* or *imitari*

tinctis . . . capillis Jokes about men and women who dye their hair or wear wigs (cf. 1.72) are part of the repertoire of physical humor in Martial and other Latin writers.

2 **corvus . . . cycnus** The metaphor evokes the contrast between these birds' colors, black and white respectively.

3 **scit te . . . canum** As often, the infinitive *esse* is understood in this indirect statement.

Proserpina Daughter of Ceres (in Greek: Persephone, daughter of Demeter), she was carried off by Hades, king of the underworld, to be his wife. In a story most famously told in the *Homeric Hymn to Demeter,* Demeter eventually forced a pact to the effect that Hades could have her daughter for only part of the year; Persephone's annual return to earth coincides with the arrival of spring. Because of her dual residence, her name is sometimes associated with the birth of new life in the spring, and sometimes—as here—with the realm of the dead.

4 **personam** Laetinus' technique of dyeing his hair is described not only as an act of deception (*mentiris*, line 1) but as a metaphorical stage performance: death will take off Laetinus' mask.

∾ *Book 4*

4.24

1 **quas habuit** As often, the rel. clause is inserted between its antecedent (*amicas*) and the adj. modifying it (*omnes*).

2 **extulit** lit., "has accompanied on their funeral procession." Like the comparable English expression ("she has buried all her friends"), the Latin need not be taken literally. The point is that every woman Lycoris has befriended subsequently died.

  uxori . . . meae Although this brief epigram is in the voice of a married man, we cannot conclude on this basis that Martial himself was married at the time he wrote the poem (see the Introduction for further discussion). In any case, rough jokes at the expense of wives are standard items in the cultural repertoire of masculine humor in ancient Rome and elsewhere ("take my wife—please!").

4.56

1 **munera . . . mittis** For the practice of showering rich old men and women with gifts in hopes of making it into their will or even marrying them, cf. 1.10.

2 **vis . . . vocem** i.e., *vis ut vocem*, a common ellipsis

3 **sordidius nihil est** In an *apo koinou* structure (cf. 2.22.3), the subsequent clause supplies the comparative *te*.

  uno modifying *te* ("you and you alone"), adding emphasis to *nihil*

4 **vocare** can take two acc. objects ("to call X 'Y'"); context will make clear which comes first in translation

5 **sic** "in just the same way"

  indulget i.e., "teases"

6 **callida . . . esca** a compressed expression: it is not the bait that is clever, but the human being who has set it out

  stultas . . . feras The phrase combines two prejudices about animals especially characteristic of the Western cultural tradition—

that they are unintelligent and savage—and at the same time is making a point both about Gargilianus and about those whose favor he is courting.

7   **quid sit largiri, quid sit donare** "what being generous is, what giving gifts is," i.e., what it *really* means to be generous or to give gifts. The clauses are dependent upon *docebo*.

8   **dona** imperative of the verb *donare* used, as often, absolutely (i.e., without a direct object expressed)

∾ *Book 5*

5.58

1   **te victurum** As often, the infinitive *esse* is omitted.

Postume a name applied to a range of characters in Martial's epigrams (cf. 2.21); here perhaps recalling Horace's memorable *Odes* 2.14: *eheu fugaces Postume, Postume . . .*

2   **cras istud** "that 'tomorrow' of which you speak." The key term *cras* has already appeared three times in the opening couplet and will be emphatically repeated throughout the epigram—except in the final occurrence, as a substantive and the subject of a verb.

3   **unde petendum** understand *est*: Where are we to look for it? Where can it be found?

4   **apud Parthos Armeniosque** i.e., far to the east, beyond the borders of the Roman Empire. Rome subjugated Armenia, previously a "client state," only after Martial's death, but Parthia (largely coextensive with modern Iran) never.

5   **Priami vel Nestoris annos** The geographical and cultural imagery of the preceding line is complemented by a mythological metaphor. Priam, king of Troy, and Nestor, skilled orator and adviser to the Greeks—memorable old men in Homer's *Iliad*—here and elsewhere suggest extreme old age.

6   **quanti** with *emi*, gen. of value or price

possit potential subjunctive. This is the reading of the manuscripts in family γ and printed by Shackleton Bailey in his Loeb edition, among others. Manuscripts of family β give *posset,* which is printed by Lindsay in the Oxford Classical Text.

7   **cras vives?** The question both reiterates the opening of the poem and anticipates Postumus' attempt at an answer to Martial's insistent objections. The following sentence dismisses the attempt as pointless.

serum est i.e., is already too late; an interesting qualification of the advice given at 1.15.12 (*vive hodie*)

5.81

1   **Aemiliane** a common name. Note the pattern of the word-initial sounds in this line (*s-p-e-s-p-e-ae*), the syntactical repetition with variation (*pauper eris ~ pauper es*), and the roughly chiastic pattern of word-initial sounds in the second line (*d-o-n-n-n-d*)

2   **nullis . . . nisi divitibus** a typical double negative: "to no people if not to the rich," i.e., *only* to the rich

nunc an important detail. Martial is not only describing a phenomenon bemoaned in Juvenal's third satire—if a rich man loses his home and possessions to a fire, his friends and family will help him replace them, whereas a poor man in a similar situation becomes even poorer—but is also taking part in a long tradition of lamenting cultural decline: today is worse than yesterday.

5.83

1   Note the arrangement of the opening four words, given particularly lapidary quality by the omission of the implied conjs. (*si/dum/cum insequeris* and *si/dum/cum fugis*): in fact, there is not a single conj. or prep. in this swift and compressed couplet. These four words rapidly sketch a scenario familiar from a wide range of Greek and Latin poetry beginning with the archaic poets Theognis and Sappho: the complexities of desire in general and of erotic pursuit in particular. As often, Ovid's poetry may have provided a specific model: cf. *Amores* 2.19.36 (*quod sequitur, fugio; quod fugit, ipse sequor*).

2   **velle tuum** The infinitive, by definition a verbal noun, is here
    modified by the possessive adj. and functioning as the direct ob-
    ject of the verb *nolo*; similarly with *nolle* (sc. *tuum*). This usage
    of the infinitive may have been colloquial: cf. Petronius *Satyri-
    con* 52.3 (*meum intellegere*).

    Dindyme The name suggests a slave from Asia Minor, since
    Dindymos is a mountain associated with the cult of Cybele
    and thus also with her eunuch priests, the *galli*. Martial uses
    it in other epigrams to refer to desirable young male slaves or
    eunuchs.

∾ *Book 6*

6.1

METER: Phalaecian hendecasyllable

1   **sextus . . . libellus** The incorporation of explicit references to
    book numbers within poetic compositions is characteristic of
    Martial. For his poetry's tendency to thematize itself and its
    readers, cf. 1.1–1.3.

    mittitur The scenario imagined is that this poem accompanies
    an edition of Book 6 being sent to Martialis.

2   **in primis** an idiomatic expression, sometimes printed as one
    word with assimilation (*imprimis*): "among the first," i.e., espe-
    cially, particularly, above all

    Martialis cf. 1.15.1

3   **quem** the antecedent is *libellus*

    terseris lit., "wipe off, clean," i.e., polish up and correct, a favor
    Martial asks of friends in some other epigrams as well

    aure diligenti The reference to the ear rather than the eye (un-
    expected, even awkward, after *terseris*) reminds us of the wide-
    spread ancient practice of reading texts aloud.

4   **minus anxius tremensque** personification of the book of po-
    etry: cf. 1.2, 1.3

5   **magnas** either a transferred epithet (equivalent to *magni Caesaris in manus*) or a rhetorical gesture of flattery (Domitian is so godlike that even his hands are grander than those of ordinary mortals)

    Caesaris cf. spect.1.7. Martial periodically advertises the possibility that the emperor is one of his readers.

6.34

1   **basia da nobis** With these opening words—and especially when the question of *how many* kisses is raised (*quot*)—many readers will hear an allusion to Catullus (cf. Catullus 5.7–8: *da mi basia mille, deinde centum, / dein mille altera . . .*). The intertextuality becomes explicit in the final couplet.

    Diadumene Like Dindymos (5.83.2), the name suggests a young male slave, and in addition may evoke Greek ideals of youthful male beauty, since one of the fifth-century BCE sculptor Polykleitos' most famous statues was known as the *Diadumenos* ("tying his hair with a band").

    pressa the pple. suggests both "strong and passionate" and "in quick succession"

2-3   The lines evoke and vary Catullan imagery for innumerable kisses: the sands of the Libyan desert and the stars in the sky (7), or ears of grain in a field (48).

    Oceani referring to the Atlantic, as opposed to the Mediterranean and its various branches (such as the Aegean Sea mentioned in the following verse)

3   **sparsas per litora conchas** cf. Ovid *Ars amatoria* 2.519: *litore quot conchae, tot sunt in amore dolores*

4   **Cecropio monte** Mount Hymettus above Athens, known for the excellent honey produced by its bees (cf. 13.108); Cecrops was the first king in Attica

5   **quaeque sonant** *quae,* with *ea* as implied antecedent, is the direct object of *sonant*, whose subject is *vocesque manusque*: "the sounds which the voices and hands make" (for *-que . . . -que* cf. 1.15.7).

6   **subiti Caesaris** i.e., when the emperor makes an unexpected appearance in the theater's audience. The culmination of the list of natural phenomena with a pseudo-theophany of Domitian not only flatters him, but reminds us of an important difference between the sociopolitical contexts in which Catullus and Martial were writing.

7   **quot** i.e., *basia*

     arguto cf. 1.1.3

     exorata modifying *Lesbia*; for the meaning of the verb, see the note on 1.6.3.

8   **cupit** The subject is expressed by the subsequent clause: (*is*) *qui . . . potest*. The point is that if you are capable of keeping track of the number of kisses, you want relatively few; Martial's desires are on another scale.

ꙮ *Book 7*

7.5

1   **populique patrumque** Since *patres* (*conscripti*) was an honorific title for Senators, the expression is a reversed rephrasing of the traditional *senatus populusque Romanus*.

2   **respicis** i.e., take into consideration (cf. the English derivative "with respect to"). The verb is often used in prayers to a god to look favorably upon a human request.

     Latiae . . . togae The toga bore an enormous symbolic weight as the characteristic garment of the male Roman citizen (cf. Vergil *Aeneid* 1.282: *Romanos rerum dominos gentemque togatam*). Martial's phrase is a metonymy for the entire citizen body.

3   **deum**, i.e., yourself. Domitian infamously had himself referred to in official documents as *dominus et deus noster* (Suetonius *Domitian* 13). Suetonius calls this *arrogantia,* but the language was not as shocking in a Roman context as it seems today. Although Roman practice since the time of Augustus had been to officially deify emperors only after their death, there was a long

poetic and rhetorical tradition, likewise beginning with Augustus, of using the language of divinity to describe living emperors.

votis is abl. of means dependent upon *poscentibus*, which is m. dat. pl. of the substantivized pple., to be taken with *redde*. In other words, Domitian is being asked to answer the people's prayers that he might return safely to Rome. The epigram seems to have been written during an eight-month campaign that Domitian led against the Sarmatians; he eventually returned to Rome in January 93 CE.

invidet hosti / Roma suo a paradox: why would Rome ever envy its barbarian enemies? The answer comes in the next and final couplet of the epigram.

4   **veniat . . . licet** cf. 2.23.1.

laurea metonymy for the tablets adorned with laurel leaves that were traditionally sent from a military campaign to the Senate in Rome in order to announce a victory

5   **terrarum dominum** an epithet for both gods and extraordinary human beings like the emperor

ille, i.e., *hostis*

6   **terretur . . . et fruitur** homoioteleuton with variety: the verbs belong to different conjugations, and the second is deponent. The two verbs frame the final line and express a mild paradox: the foreign enemy (for *barbarus* see spect.1.1) is terrified at the sight of the Roman emperor but at the same time fortunate to behold him.

7.10

1   **pedicatur Eros, fellat Linus** These blunt words introduce a series of gossipy vignettes using pseudonyms and offering an overview of the kinds of things for which Roman men might be criticized or ridiculed, perhaps behind their back. In the first line, Eros and Linus are said to perform two sexual roles considered shaming or feminizing for men (cf. 2.28). Their names may well have ironic overtones, since they also refer to mythic characters: Eros is the Greek equivalent of Cupid, and Linus is the son of Apollo.

Ole, quid ad te understand a verb like *est, attinet*, or (cf. line 9) *pertinet*: "What does it matter to you?" This phrase initiates a series of repetitions at the end of the first line of each of the first five couplets, taking a clear stance in response to Olus' participation in gossip. *Olus* was a popular pronunciation of the name *Aulus* (cf. *Claudius/Clodius*).

2   **de cute . . . sua** i.e., with his own body

3   **centenis futuit . . . milibus** understand, as often, gen. pl. *sestertium* (cf. 2.44.7). Put less bluntly, Matho spends a great deal of money on female prostitutes. By way of contextualizing the amount: a man needed to have a minimum of four hundred thousand sesterces in assets to be able to join the equestrian order (*equites*), at least one million in order to become a senator.

5   **in lucem** i.e., all through the night and into the following day

6   **tota . . . nocte** Not only the acc. but also the abl. could be used to denote extent of time. The abl. is far more common in the language of epitaphs, where one regularly finds formulaic phrases such as *vixit LXX annis*.

7   **septingenta** understand *milia* (cf. 2.30.1) *sestertium* (cf. line 3): a considerable amount (see note on line 3)

8   **assem** see note on 2.44.9

     ne dederis crediderisve *ne* + pf. subjunctive is one means of expressing a negative imperative. In a financial context, the verb *credere* means "to give a loan to"; cf. the English derivatives "credit" and "creditor."

9   **ad te quod pertinet** the rel. pron. is postponed and its antecedent is *illud*. With this couplet the refrain switches from the question "What does it matter to you?" to a series of fairly devastating assertions about what *should* matter to Olus. Note that the speaker hardly responds to Olus' penchant for gossip by refusing to engage in gossipmongering of his own!

10   **curae convenit esse tuae** i.e., *curae convenit esse tibi* (double dative): "what should be a matter of concern to you"

12   **quadrantem** cf. 2.44.9

13　**moecha** A Greek borrowing, more or less equivalent to Latin *adultera*, referring to a married woman who has sexual relations with someone other than her husband, and consequently a strong insult in Rome's patriarchal society.

　　tibi dat. of reference, equivalent to *tua* ("your wife is a *moecha*"), or else dat. of possession, taken with *est* ("you have a *moecha* for a wife")

14　**dotem** money and/or possessions given by a bride's father to the man whom she marries

　　grandis i.e., of marriageable age, which for Romans was generally marked by the onset of menstruation

15　**quindecies** probably not literal but signifying, like English "a dozen," an indefinite but substantial number; cf. 11.6.3, *quindecim poetae*

　　poteram cf. 1.3.12 for the tense

16　**nihil** as often, adverbial: "in no way, not at all." Its position as the poem's final word and its isolation by means of the final iteration of the vocative *Ole* give the word all the more emphasis.

7.14

1　**accidit** The context (especially *amisit* in the following line) makes it clear that this is pf., not pres.

　　Aule This is probably the Aulus Pudens to whom Martial dedicates a number of epigrams throughout his collection, but even most ancient readers of this poem would not have known who he was. The vocative adds a note of liveliness by evoking a scene in which we overhear Martial making a witty remark to a friend.

2　**amisit** as often, a euphemism referring to the loss of someone close to death (cf. 1.33.1)

　　lusus deliciasque "her playmate, her darling." Who exactly this is does not become clear until the poem's final couplet.

3　**quales** pl. since its antecedents *lusus deliciasque* are grammatically pl.; but the referent is to one person

teneri . . . amica Catulli Catullus 2 and 3 describe Lesbia's playful sparrow and her mourning at the bird's death (for *amica* cf. 2.62.3). In general, elegiac poetry on erotic themes describes itself as soft (*mollis*) and tender (*tener*), and the same qualities— the opposite of a rough, hard masculinity—could be attributed to the poets themselves.

5   **Stellae . . . meo** dat. of agent with the pf. pass. pple. *cantata*, a frequent construction in Latin poetry; *meus* is a way of affectionately referring to a friend or relative. Both Martial and Statius describe the poet Lucius Arruntius Stella as an important supporter and patron.

Ianthis the Greek pseudonym for his wife that Stella used in his poetry, one theme of which was the death of her pet dove. An epigram of Martial's from Book 1 asserts that Stella's dove surpasses Catullus' sparrow (1.7).

7   **lux mea** a common term of endearment along with *mea vita, meum desiderium, mi ocelle,* and others

capitur "is captivated, caught"

8   **dominae** understand *meae*

9   **bis senos . . . annos** a common type of periphrasis using the distributive instead of the cardinal: "two groups of six" for "twelve." The manuscripts, and with them Lindsay's Oxford Classical Text, read *bis denos* ("twice ten"), but most modern editors print the emendation *bis senos,* since the following line makes much more sense if the boy is twelve rather than twenty years old. On the other hand, the final joke shows that numbers in this poem cannot be taken literally, and a twenty-year-old slave could easily be called a *puer.*

10   **mentula** After the the measured, formal language of the preceding couplets and their extended evocation of Catullus' lyric poetry, this primary obscenity (cf. 1.34.10, 1.35.4) comes as quite a surprise at the beginning of the poem's final line. The word bluntly reminds us that we are, after all, reading epigram, a genre which, as Martial repeatedly reminds us, claimed the

use of obscenity as one of its perquisites. There may be more to the joke than that, since many of Catullus' readers over the centuries have seen phallic symbolism in Lesbia's sparrow—apparently including Martial himself (cf. 11.6.14–16, addressed to an attractive slave: *da nunc basia, sed Catulliana: / quae si tot fuerint quot ille dixit, / donabo tibi passerem Catulli*).

sesquipedalis "a foot and a half." In all its comic exaggeration, and as is often the case with jokes, this final remark reveals some cultural preoccupations: an interest in unusually large penises is a recurring theme in the Latin textual and visual tradition.

ꙮ *Book 8*

8.12

1   **ducere** understand *in matrimonium,* the standard phrase for describing a man's taking a wife (cf. 1.24.4). Martial writes sometimes in the voice of a married man (in 11.43, for example, he describes how his wife has caught him in bed with a slave-boy), sometimes—as here—in that of a bachelor with quite strong views on women and marriage.

2   **quaeritis?** The question-and-answer structure is a common opening or closing device in Martial's epigrams (cf. 2.17 and 2.26 among others). The scenario could be either that of a man in conversation with a group of friends or that of the poet Martial addressing his anonymous readership (cf. 1.2, 1.3).

    nubere nolo The final *-o* is counted as short (cf. 1.24.4). The verb *nubere* takes the dat. and refers to the role of the bride in a Roman wedding ceremony (cf. *nubes,* "veil"). The phrase thus stands in balanced contrast with *ducere nolim* in the preceding line, and the alliteration draws attention to the paradox: "I do not want to be my wife's wife."

3   This rather brutally formulates a traditional hierarchical view of the relationship between husband and wife: the speaker rejects the possibility of marrying a woman wealthier than himself because it would place her in an intolerably dominant position.

Prisce This may be Terentius Priscus, a friend and supporter whom Martial names in several books, but Priscus is a fairly common name and certainty is not possible. In any case knowledge of who he is and what he is like will have been limited to very few of Martial's contemporary readers.

4　non aliter "not otherwise," i.e., this is the only way

pares The adj. evokes an ideal of balance within a relationship in which the husband has the dominant position; non-hierarchical equality is not at stake here. The ideal of *concordia* between husband and wife, evoked throughout the Latin literary tradition and in epitaphs as well, coexisted with hierarchical models for gendered roles within marriage.

8.17

1　egi . . . tuam . . . causam This is the only poem in Martial's oeuvre in the voice of a man who has represented someone else in a legal proceeding; otherwise Martial contrasts his own status as relatively poor poet with that of wealthy *causidici* (cf. 2.30, 12.68). See the Introduction for discussion of the varying perspectives and occasional self-contradictions in the persona we find in Martial's poetry.

pactus pf. pass. pple. of *paciscor*

duo milia understand *sestertium* (cf. 2.30.1). Note the alliteration of *mi-* in this verse, continuing *milia* from the first verse.

2　misisti . . . quod the conj. is postponed: "[as for the fact] that you sent . . ." Note the parallel between the verse-initial verb and *egi* in the preceding line, continued with *narrasti* at the start of the next.

nummos lit., "coins," often used as a synonym for sesterces in particular. Sextus has paid only half of the agreed-upon amount.

3　narrasti syncopated pf. (= *narravisti*) of a type common in Latin of all periods and styles. *Narratio* was a technical term for that part of a courtroom speech in which the speaker gave his version of what happened; Sextus is accusing Martial of having mounted such an inadequate defence that he did not even attempt to do this.

4　**debes** understand *mihi*. Why Martial can paradoxically assert that Sextus owes him money for having *lost* the case becomes clear in what follows.

quod erubui "because I blushed," i.e., I was too ashamed to speak about it. The implication is that whatever Sextus did, it was both so disgraceful and so undeniable that the only technique Martial could use was to adopt an embarrassed silence—whether in the slim hope that this might win the jurors' sympathy, or out of sheer helplessness.

8.23

2　**propter cenam** i.e., because of an unsatisfactorily cooked or presented dinner

Rustice probably not a coincidental name, hinting at a contrast between country and city life, the latter filled with banquets, slaves, and demanding masters

caedo cocum For the scansion of the verb, cf. 1.24.4. In view of their importance both to daily life and to the social standing of Roman slave-owners, who were constantly exchanging dinner invitations and hosting parties, good cooks were highly prized and could be quite expensive.

3　**levis** i.e., insufficiently serious, trivial

4　**ex qua . . . causa** "for what reason"

vis . . . vapulet i.e., *vis ut vapulet* (cf. 4.56.2). It is hard to read the tone of this final line, key to the characterization of the speaker. On the most straightforward reading, the persona is that of the poet himself, who poses the question in all seriousness: if you can't beat a cook for having ruined a meal, what can you beat him for? Alternatively, the speaker is a character from whom the poet creates an ironic distance, implicitly commenting on the trivial grounds he gives for beating his slave. Another epigram (2.66) harshly criticizes a woman who has beaten her slave-girl with a mirror after she inadequately pinned down a lock of hair, and writers like Seneca and Juvenal also attack those who abuse their slaves. It is important to note, however, that no text from ancient Rome suggests abolishing slavery itself. At most it is a question of how to treat one's slaves, and this epigram reminds us of the kinds of things that slaves might be up against.

8.55

1   **temporibus nostris** dat. with *cedat*

  cum cedat causal. The claim stands in tension with a paradigm we find throughout the Greek and Latin textual tradition: that of steady decline since a lost Golden Age (cf. 5.81). The following verse gives one justification for the model of progress.

2   **creverit et** postponed *et*; the verb is parallel to *cedat* (note the different tenses of the subjunctive)

  cum duce . . . suo i.e., the emperor Domitian

3   **sacri . . . Maronis** Roman men could be identified by their praenomen, nomen, or cognomen alone—thus Cicero could be referred to simply as *Tullius* (9.70.1) or Vergil as *Maro*—or in various combinations (cf. 12.3.3). The adj. *sacer* does not always have the same connotations as English "holy" or "sacred" and here is closer to the sense of "revered" (cf. 1.93.5). In any case, Vergil was held in great esteem even before his death.

  desse contracted from *de-esse*

4   **tanta bella sonare tuba** The meter reveals which noun the adj. modifies. To unpack the metaphor: Flaccus is surprised that no one today is composing epic poetry on warfare with such grand effect as Vergil.

5   A memorable line with the quality of a *sententia*. **sint**: jussive subjunctive; *derunt* is contracted from *de-erunt*. In effect, *sint . . . non derunt* is equivalent to a fut. more vivid condition (*si erunt . . . non derunt*).

Maecenates referring to C. Cilnius Maecenas, the powerful friend of Augustus and supporter or patron of a number of poets, including Vergil and Horace; for the pl., cf. 1.24.3. One form that Maecenas' support of poets took—in addition to introducing them to Augustus—is the topic of the rest of this epigram.

Flacce a friend and supporter whom Martial names throughout his epigrams; as this poem makes clear, he is in a financial position to function as a modern-day Maecenas. Martial's choice to address this poem to him may not be coincidental, since *Flaccus* was also the poet Horace's cognomen (cf. 12.3.1).

6   **vel tua rura** Flaccus came from the area of Padua (1.61) and Martial's point seems to be "even a remote country region like Flaccus' homeland could produce a Vergil, if there were a Maecenas to support him" (Watson and Watson).

7   **perdiderat** The subject is expressed in the following clause (*apo koinou*: cf. 2.22.3).

Since *Cremona* had supported Brutus, after the latter's defeat at Philippi in 42 BCE Octavian confiscated much of the surrounding territory and awarded it to his own veterans and supporters. According to tradition, Vergil himself was among those whose land was confiscated (though this may be a false deduction from his poetry; cf. Vergil *Eclogues* 9.28: *Mantua vae miserae nimium vicina Cremonae*) and he was subsequently rescued from financial difficulty by Maecenas. Martial's couplet (re-)interprets in autobiographical terms Vergil's first and ninth *Eclogues,* in which we read of the shepherd *Tityrus'* loss of land.

8   **flebat et** postponed conj.

  aeger not physically ill, but "sick at heart, desperate"

9   **risit** suggesting Maecenas' (perhaps quasi-divine) effortless superiority in solving Vergil's problem

  Tuscus eques a periphrasis for Maecenas, who belonged to the equestrian order and whose descent from ancient Etruscan royalty is prominently celebrated at the opening of Horace's first book of *Odes* (Horace *Odes* 1.1.1: *Maecenas atavis edite regibus*).

12   **tu licet et . . . ames** = *et licet (ut) tu ames.* Both the postponement of the conj. *et* and the omission of *ut* with *licet* (cf. 2.23.1) are common.

nostrum . . . Alexin The beautiful young Alexis in Vergil's second *Eclogue,* desperately desired by Corydon, was said to have been inspired by a slave named Alexander, who was given to Vergil as a gift, either (as Martial writes) by Maecenas or by Asinius Pollio. Once again the boundary between poetic fiction and biographical fact is blurred: as Tityrus = Vergil, so Alexis = Alexander.

13   **adstabat . . . mensis** Alexis was given a task often reserved for attractive young slaves: serving food and pouring wine at meals.

domini In view of the impf. tenses, this is probably Maecenas, but might possibly be the slave's new master Vergil.

14   **marmorea** The adj. evokes the creamy color of marble. Many Romans prized a pale complexion in the objects of their desire, whether male or female; see note on 1.72.5.

nigra Falerna probably poetic pl.; alternatively, the pl. suggests repeated servings of wine. Along with the *Caecubum* and the *Opimianum,* the *Falernum* was among the most highly valued of wines; it was named after a district renowned for its excellent vineyards on the border of Latium and Campania. Martial's words evoke an aesthetic contrast between the color of Alexis' hands (*marmorea*) as he holds the wine jar and the dark liquid (*nigra*) he pours out of it.

15   **libata . . . roseis . . . labris** That a favorite servant might take a sip of the wine before pouring it or handing the cup to his master is a commonplace of Latin poetry on the topic of beautiful slaves. The adj. continues the aesthetic exploration of colors.

16   **quae poterant** As the context makes clear, the antecedent is *labris*; for the tense of the verb, cf. 1.3.12.

ipsum sollicitare Iovem The verb suggests not only physical stimulation but also the imagery of disturbance or anxiety often associated with erotic desire in Latin poetry (cf. the key term *cura*). This clause indirectly refers to Ganymede (cf. 1.6), to whom beautiful young male slaves were regularly compared.

17 **excidit attonito . . . poetae** dat. with compound verb; dazzled by Alexis' beauty, Vergil dropped all thoughts of Galatea or Thestylis

pinguis Galatea . . . /Thestylis et postponed conj.; the names refer to two female characters in Vergil's *Eclogues*, the former lovers of Tityrus and Corydon respectively.

18 **rubras . . . genas** retained acc. (or acc. of respect) with the pf. pass. pple. *usta*. The image is of a woman sunburned from working all day in the fields; the contrast with Alexis' creamy skin is as unflattering to Thestylis as the adj. *pinguis* is to Galatea.

19 **Italiam concepit et "Arma virumque"** The context makes it clear that the subject is Vergil. *Arma virumque* are the opening words of the *Aeneid*, famous in antiquity and found, for example, scratched on numerous walls in Pompeii. There is some debate, however, as to the specific reference of *Italiam*. Either it is a synecdoche for the *Georgics,* alluding to the famous passage known as the *laudes Italiae* (*Georgics* 2.136–176), or else it is a reference to the *Aeneid*, the second half of which takes place in Italy, in which case the entire line refers to the *Aeneid*.

20 **Culicem** a witty poem on the death of a gnat attributed (probably falsely) to the young Vergil and included in a collection of texts called the *Appendix Vergiliana*

21 **quid . . . loquar** deliberate subjunctive

Varios Marsosque for the pl., cf. 1.24.3. Varius Rufus, friend of both Vergil and Horace and like them supported by Maecenas, composed epic poetry and drama and was best known for his now-lost tragedy *Thyestes*. His contemporary Domitius Marsus published a collection of epigrams called *Cicuta* ("Hemlock"), presumably because of their vitriolic or poisonous tone. In the preface to Book 1 Martial names Marsus, Catullus, Pedo, and Gaetulicus as examples of epigrammatists whose works have a wide readership.

ditataque vatum / nomina transferred epithet; it is not the poets' names but the poets themselves who became wealthy

22   **quos numerare** antecedent is *vatum*. The rel. clause is in apposition to *magnus labor*: "to name them all will be a huge effort."

23   **ergo ero Vergilius** Note the sudden shift of focus to Martial himself, picking up on the hint to Flaccus in line 6 and in the end giving specificity to an epigram that until now seems to be making a more general point.

24   By means of its surprise ending (we might expect Martial to say "I will be a second Vergil") this poem reiterates a recurring theme in Martial: his poetry is different from tragedy and epic. The closing words invoke a long tradition known as *recusatio*, whereby a poet elegantly refuses a request (e.g., to celebrate Caesar's victories or write epic poetry).

❧ *Book 9*

9.praef.

mi Torani mentioned on only one other occasion in Martial's oeuvre (5.78); for *mi* cf. 7.14.5. Five of Martial's fifteen books (1, 2, 8, 9, 12) come with a prose preface, as do all five books of Statius' *Silvae*.

frater carissime The non-literal use of *frater* and *soror* as terms of endearment was widespread, attested not only by a broad range of literary texts but also by letters written at a Roman outpost at Vindolanda in northern England. In the case of relationships between men, the usage reflects a conceptual overlap between two of the most highly valued of relationships in Roman culture: male friendship and brotherly love.

extra ordinem paginarum i.e., the epigram that follows was positioned separately from the body of Book 9. The word *pagina* refers either to a page in the modern sense (i.e., a leaf of a codex edition: cf. 1.2) or to a column of text in a papyrus scroll.

Stertinium probably Lucius Stertinius Avitus, consul suffect in 92 CE and likewise a poet; cf. 1.16.2

clarissimum virum a standard phrase of polite respect to describe an upper-class man, often specifically denoting senatorial rank

imaginem meam The noun can refer to a portrait in a variety of media: an ancestral mask, a statue or bust, or (as seems to be the case here) a painting.

scribendum tibi understand *esse*. The context makes it clear that there is an implied dat. of agent *mihi* and that *tibi* is the indirect object.

Avitus iste quis vocaretur i.e., *quis sit iste Avitus qui vocaretur* (the verb means "addressed in the poem that follows")

para hospitium The phrase signals that Martial is planning a trip to visit Toranius.

1   **note** vocative sing., modifying *vates*

     licet nolis for the syntax, cf. 2.23.1; understand *esse notus*

2   **serus . . . cinis** in other words, you will live a long life; cf. 1.1.6 for this metonymic use of *cinis*

3   **tibi . . . vivat** ethical date and jussive subjunctive; i.e., may it continue to exist for your enjoyment

4   **non obscuris** litotes, i.e., "renowned"

5   **ille ego sum** a formulaic phrase in dedicatory verse; cf. Ovid *Amores* 2.1.1–2: *Hoc quoque composui Paelignis natus aquosis, / ille ego nequitiae Naso poeta meae.* A probably spurious opening to the *Aeneid* transmitted in some manuscripts begins thus: *Ille ego qui quondam gracili modulatus avena . . .*

     nulli take with *secundus* ("second to none")

     nugarum objective gen. with *laude*, a term of ironically modest self-description standard in light poetry such as Catullus' shorter poems or Martial's epigrams

6   **non miraris sed . . . amas** The veneer of modesty wears particularly thin here and in other such declarations found throughout Martial's poetry: I may be no Vergil, but people read me!

     lector For the importance of the anonymous reader in Martial's poetry, see Introduction and cf. 1.1.

7   **maiora sonent** "make louder, grander sounds"; compare the
     common Latin metaphor of poetry as song

     mihi . . . locuto take with *sufficit* in the next line

     parva n. acc. pl., direct object of *locuto*. There is thus a balanced
     contrast between *maiora sonent* and *parva locuto*.

8   **sufficit** plus dat. and infinitive: "it is enough for me to . . .," i.e.,
     "I am satisfied if . . ."

     vestras Note the shift from the sing. *lector* in line 6 to this pl.,
     a subtle reminder that Martial claims a widespread readership
     throughout the Latin-speaking world

9.15

1   **inscripsit** i.e., caused an epitaph to be inscribed. Nearly 400,000
     Latin inscriptions surviving from antiquity have been tran-
     scribed and published, and about 300,000 of them commemo-
     rate the dead, often naming the person who commissioned the
     tomb and/or epitaph.

Fig. 4. Epitaph above the entrance to tomb n. 86 of the Isola Sacra necropolis near
Ostia. The text announces that the freedwoman Clodia Prepusa has dedicated
this tomb to herself and to her husband L. Clodius Atimetus, as well as to her own
freedmen and freedwomen and their descendants. Photograph by Craig Williams.

scelerata In some epitaphs, this adj. describes parents who survive their children: "ill-starred" or "accursed," perhaps also expressing self-reproach for outliving the deceased (cf. *Corpus Inscriptionum Latinarum* 6.15160: *filiis suis infelicissimis . . . fecit mater scelerata*). Martial's use of the adj. to describe Chloe is pointedly ambivalent; the next line implies that she may have been *scelerata* in another sense.

2 **se fecisse** indirect statement with *inscripsit*. The direct statement in the epitaphs would have been something like *ipsa feci* ("I myself have dedicated this tomb to my husband").

quid pote simplicius? understand *esse*: "What could possibly be more straightforward than that?" What indeed? Precisely behind the simplicity both of Chloe's epitaphs and of Martial's final question lies a dark ambiguity, since *ipsa feci* could also be taken to mean "I did it myself," i.e., I killed them myself. The husband-killer was a significant stereotype in Greek and Roman images of women, from monumental mythic figures like Clytemnestra to contemporary women who might be the subject of perhaps anxious jokes like this.

9.70

1 **Tullius** For the use of the nomen rather than the cognomen, cf. 8.55.3. Martial is referring to Cicero's famous exclamation at the opening of his speech to the Senate in 63 BCE in which he denounced what he claimed was a revolutionary conspiracy led by L. Sergius Catilina. Cicero's actual words are *o tempora! o mores!* (*Cat.* 1.2; also quoted by Seneca the Elder, *Suasoriae* 6.3, and Quintilian, *Institutio Oratoria* 9.2.26). Martial has reversed the order so as to fit the dactylic meter.

2 **sacrilegum . . . nefas** The strong language of moral condemnation reproduces Cicero's perspective. As it happens, Cicero's four speeches against Catiline are peppered with the language of *nefas* (especially the adj. *nefarius*) but the word *sacrilegus* does not occur: Martial has outdone Cicero!

3   **gener atque socer** Pompey the Great and Julius Caesar respec-
     tively. Caesar had given his daughter Julia in marriage to Pom-
     pey in order to solidify their alliance (Martial's phrase may have
     been inspired by Catullus 29.24: *socer generque, perdidistis om-*
     nia). Since Caesar and Pompey came into open conflict more
     than a decade after the events surrounding Catiline, Martial
     seems to be conflating two major events of that turbulent period
     in Roman history. On the other hand, Cicero used the phrase *o*
     tempora! o mores! in other speeches both before and after 63 BCE,
     including his defence of King Deiotarus, who had sided with
     Pompey against Caesar and was put on trial in 45 BCE (*pro rege*
     Deiotaro 31; see also *in Verrem* 2.4.56 and *de Domo sua* 137).

     concurreret When the subject is compound ("A and B"), subject-
     verb agreement is looser in written Latin than it is in written Mod-
     ern English: the verb may be pl., agreeing with both nouns, or it
     may agree with the second noun only (in this case the sing. *socer*).

4   **maesta** The earth is implicitly personified, grieving as it is be-
     spattered with Roman blood drawn by other Romans.

     civili caede maderet An especially compressed phrase: the noun
     is used metonymically for blood (*caede = sanguine, cruore*),
     while the adj. means "shed in civil war."

6   **quod tibi non placeat** rel. clause of characteristic, preceding its
     antecedent (the interrog. *quid*)

7–8 **nulla ducum feritas** The phrase might imply the excesses of the
     military leaders of the late Republic (e.g., the proscriptions of
     Sulla in 82 BCE) and/or of emperors like Nero (cf. spect.2.3: *feri*
     . . . regis). In any case, Martial is reproducing traditional pro-
     paganda according to which Augustus put an end to over 100
     years of civil strife at Rome and subsequent *principes*—at least
     the good ones—assured the continuance of peace. Skeptical
     observers, both ancient and modern, have seen this as a thinly
     veiled justification for autocracy.

9   **nostri** The noun to which this adj. refers only becomes clear in
     the following line (*apo koinou*). The implicit contrast is thus *non*
     nostri mores sed mores tui.

faciunt tibi quod . . . sordent "cause them to seem sordid to you," "make them not good enough for you"

10 **tui** This final word drives the point of the epigram smoothly home. This man's complaints about the decadence of contemporary society have nothing to do with social realities or historical change and everything to do with him.

ᔌ *Book 10*

10.4

1–2 The opening couplet lists four mythological characters—two male, two female—who figured in epic and tragic poetry and who, as Martial concludes at the end of the couplet, were renowned for their monstrous deeds, all of which involved the violation or inversion of relationships with kin. *Oedipus*, king of Thebes, unwittingly fulfilled a prophecy that he would kill his father and marry his mother, and (in the most famous telling of his tale, Sophocles' play *Oedipus the King*) subsequently blinded himself as an act of self-punishment. *Thyestes* robbed his brother Atreus of both wife and throne at Mycenae; Atreus took his dreadful revenge by killing Thyestes' sons and feeding their corpses to him in a stew. On the advice of an oracle, Thyestes later mated with his own daughter Pelopia in order to produce a further son—Aegisthus—who would eventually kill Atreus' son Agamemnon. Although *caligantem*, "blinded," might seem more appropriate as an epithet for Oedipus, the adjective apparently evokes Thyestes' mental blindness as he ate his own children, perhaps also with an allusion to the story that the horrified sun hid itself in an eclipse. *Colchidas* (for the pl. cf. 1.24.3) refers to Medea, daughter of the king of Colchis on the far eastern shores of the Black Sea (present-day Georgia); she killed her own children by Jason in order to make him suffer after he abandoned her for the young princess of Corinth. *Scyllas* (again a generic pl.) probably refers to the daughter of king Nisos, who betrayed her father in an unsuccessful attempt to win the heart of the Cretan king Minos, but might also suggest the monstrous creature of the same name, in the *Odyssey* and elsewhere paired with Charybdis at the straits of Messina.

monstra i.e., monstrous or horrific deeds and characters

3   **quid tibi** The verb comes in the next line.

3-4 The second couplet names four more mythological figures, not doers of monstrous deeds but beautiful young men who met an unhappy end. *Hylas* accompanied his lover Hercules on the voyage of the Argo but was lured away by nymphs and never returned, prompting a desperate and fruitless search by Hercules. *Parthenopaeus*, whose Greek name means "maiden-faced," was one of the famous Seven against Thebes who died in the attack on the city; some detect an indirect allusion to Martial's contemporary Statius (whom he never names or otherwise directly refers to), since the beautiful young Parthenopaeus is a character in his *Thebaid. Attis* of Phrygia in Asia Minor became the lover of the mother goddess Cybele; after he was unfaithful to her, she drove him insane and caused him to castrate himself (cf. 1.35, 14.204). The moon goddess (in Greek Selene, in Latin Luna) fell in love with *Endymion* when she saw him sleeping and asked Zeus to keep him permanently in that state. In some tellings of the story, the request was made by the god Sleep or by Endymion himself, but in any case Endymion's sleep was proverbial, as the noun *dormitor* (perhaps coined by Martial) suggests.

5-6 The third couplet refers to two more young men of Greek myth who met premature deaths. The first is *Icarus*, son of Daedalus, not named but immediately recognizable by the phrase *pinnis labentibus*: his father fashioned wings of feathers and wax, and the two of them set off to escape Crete by flying across the area of the Aegean Sea. Failing to heed his father's warning, Icarus flew too close to the sun; the wax melted, the wings fell off, he plunged into the area of the Aegean sea that thereafter bore his name, and so drowned. *Hermaphroditus* was the son of Hermes and Aphrodite; the water-nymph Salmacis unsuccessfully attempted to rape him but managed to merge their two bodies (hence intersexed people were called *hermaphroditi*). The oxymoronic juxtaposition *odit amatrices* emphasizes the young man's rejection of the nymph's advances, and *amatrices*—either an adj. or a noun in apposition to *aquas*—may have negative connotations, comparable to those of "hussy."

7   **vana** suggests the uselessness of mythological poetry, its distance from real life

    miserae ludibria chartae The gen. is either objective (mockeries *of* the paper on which this kind of poetry is written) or descriptive (mockeries *consisting of* that paper).

8   **quod** "with respect to which"

    vita the key to Martial's self-advertisement: his poetry, unlike that which he has just summarized, is connected with real people's real lives

9   **Centauros . . . Gorgonas Harpyiasque** Expanding upon the earlier lists of human characters, Martial now cites three typical examples of the composite beings that populate the mythic landscape: Centaurs are half-horse, half-human; Gorgons have women's bodies, but their faces are surrounded with snakes; Harpies have birds' bodies and women's heads.

10 **hominem** in emphatic contrast with the creatures just mentioned

    pagina cf. 9.praef.

    sapit "tastes like, has the flavor of." Among the wide range of metaphors used for literary style, some had to do with food and its flavors. In his brief obituary for Martial, Pliny the Younger describes his epigrams as being full of salt and bile (*Epistulae* 3.21; cf. 11.13.3 below).

11 **Mamurra** The vocative comes as a surprise to the extent that the earlier second-person forms (beginning with the opening *qui legis* and continuing through *invenies*) can easily be read as addresses to a non-specific, anonymous reader. The name is probably not coincidental, since an associate of Julius Caesar named Mamurra is harshly attacked by Catullus, who memorably calls him *non homo, sed vero mentula magna minax* (Catullus 115.8).

12 **te scire** Perhaps an allusion to one of the best known pieces of ancient Greek wisdom, prominently inscribed in the sanctuary at Delphi and made famous by Plato's Socrates: "Know yourself" (*gnōthi seauton*).

legas jussive subjunctive, a common alternative to an imperative

Callimachi famous Greek poet, scholar and critic active in third-century BCE Alexandria, whose work was influential on a variety of Roman poets. His lost *Aetia* ("Causes") consisted of four books of elegiac poetry on the origins of various cities, religious rites, and local traditions, and is here cited as an example of learned, abstruse poetry that has nothing to do with everyday human experience.

10.8

1   **nubere** cf. 1.24.4

nobis For the pl., cf. 1.35.13 and note the evidently unremarkable juxtaposition with *ego*.

ducere cf. 8.12.2. Once again, Martial writes in the persona of an unmarried man explaining why he does not want to take a certain woman as his wife.

2   **anus** the female equivalent of *senex*. In a cultural environment which placed a high value on youthful beauty, and in which the provision of children and particularly male heirs for men was an important goal of marriage, this is evidently a sufficient explanation for a man's disinclination to marry a certain woman.

si magis esset anus Typically of Martial's epigrams, this brief poem ends with a surprise and a paradox. Why would he want to marry Paula if she were even older than she already is? Those familiar with Martial's world will immediately get the joke: see 1.12, 2.26.

10.47

METER: Phalaecian hendecasyllable

1   **quae faciant** rel. clause of characteristic; the antecedent, as often, comes later (*haec*, line 2)

beatiorem The adj. suggests things ranging from contentment to material success, and signals that this poem is going to suggest a few answers to an important question asked not only in popular discourse but by a variety of philosophers (Seneca, for example, wrote an essay entitled *De beata vita*).

2   **iucundissime** a common way to address a close friend

Martialis the poet's friend Julius Martialis (cf. 1.15.1)

3   **res** As often, the noun here refers to financial resources, one's "fortune."

relicta i.e., inherited. This, the first item in Martial's catalogue, reminds us not only of the influence of Epicurean thought (according to which pleasure, understood as the absence of pain and suffering, is an ideal in itself) but also of the socioeconomic group to which this poet belonged and for which he wrote. Note, too, that this ideal stands in direct opposition to the Protestant work ethic of subsequent phases in Western culture.

4   **non ingratus ager** i.e., a productive farm. Lines 4 and 5 locate the *vita beata* at a country estate, without the countless distractions and worries of the urban existence. The contrast is a major theme in Latin literature, from Horace's tale of the country mouse and city mouse (*Satire* 2.6) to Juvenal's satires (most famously the third).

5   **toga rara** In Martial's day many Roman men wore the toga— a cumbersome, heavy woolen garment—only when they felt obliged to do so, e.g., at formal social, religious, or legal events in the city. Its rarity could thus be described as one of the delights of rustic life.

mens quieta echoing the Epicurean principle of *ataraxia* or freedom from disturbance and anxiety

6   **vires ingenuae, salubre corpus** Since the adj. *ingenuus* liter-
    ally means "free-born" as opposed to slave, this line suggests a
    combination of strength and health that is neither obtained nor
    undermined by hard physical labor.

7   **prudens simplicitas** The English derivative "simplicity" is mis-
    leading: in connection with social relations, *simplicitas* refers to
    the quality of being straightforward and direct in one's speech.
    The adj. *prudens* may suggest a tempering of such frankness
    with discretion. This, too, reflects an Epicurean ideal: that of
    friendship.

    pares amici Unlike many other interpersonal relationships in
    Roman culture (such as that between patron and client), ideal-
    ized friendship was not based on hierarchical distinctions. Mar-
    tial's phrase may suggest social parity in particular, i.e., friends
    who are of the same social class as oneself.

8   **convictus facilis** a relaxed atmosphere at dinner-parties

    sine arte mensa The food and drink served (*mensa* is metonym-
    ic) is not artificial or extravagant, as at Trimalchio's banquet in
    Petronius' *Satyricon*, but pleasing in its simplicity.

9   **non ebria, sed soluta curis** an application of the principle of
    the golden mean: there will be just enough wine to encourage
    relaxation without drunken excess

10 Now the principle of the golden mean is applied to sexual prac-
    tice: the ideal wife will not be sexually boring. As often, *tristis*
    means not "sad, unhappy," but "austere, grim"; *torus* (lit., "mar-
    riage bed") is a metonymy for sexual relations with one's spouse;
    pudicus does not mean "chaste" in the sense of "engaging in no
    sexual relations" but evokes traditional Roman ideals of sexual
    decency, above all the principle that a married woman should
    not have sexual relations with anyone other than her husband.
    In both lines 9 and 10 there may be an implicit response to the
    accusations of excessive self-indulgence and sensuality that were
    sometimes leveled against Epicureanism.

11 **qui faciat breves tenebras** i.e., the kind of sleep that causes the night to pass by quickly. This is implicitly opposed to one of the features of urban life decried by Seneca as a violation of nature (*Epistles* 122): staying up all night partying and sleeping during the daytime.

12 **quod sis** understand *id* as antecedent; the clause functions as predicate with *esse*

    velis . . . malis the main verbs of the sentence, jussive subjunctives (cf. 10.4.12)

    nihil i.e., nothing else

13 **summum . . . diem** i.e., the day of your death

    nec metuas . . . nec optes The theme of the golden mean is now applied to a fundamental question indeed—one's attitude toward one's own death—and, like much else in this poem, expresses an Epicurean ideal.

ᨓ *Book 11*

11.13

METER: Phalaecian hendecasyllable

1 **Flaminiam** understand *viam*, a major road leading out of Rome towards the north which, like many roads outside ancient cities, was lined with tombs. Roman tombs often displayed prominently located epitaphs, some of them still *in situ* on tombs along the Via dei Sepolcri outside Pompeii or in the Isola Sacra necropolis near Ostia (see Figs. 3 and 4). Some of these address the anonymous passerby as *viator* or *hospes*, asking him to stop a moment and learn who is buried there. It is not always clear whether Martial's poetic epitaphs commemorate real individuals or ponder an imaginary scenario. In this poem, we do not learn the identity of the deceased until the final line.

3 **urbis . . . Nili** Note the framing of the line by references to two very different places—the city of Rome and Egypt—and the resulting chiastic word order. Whereas a typical epitaph for a Roman

man of the upper classes lists the political offices he held in life, and that for a soldier how long he had served in the army, this line makes it clear that the person being commemorated belongs to another social group altogether: he is an entertainer from Egypt who had been popular at Rome.

sales a common metaphor for pleasurable wit (cf. 10.4.10), used by Pliny the Younger in his description of Martial's own poetry (*Epistulae* 3.21.1: *erat homo ingeniosus, acutus, acer; et qui plurimum in scribendo et salis haberet et fellis nec candoris minus*). Egyptians had a reputation for obscene humor (cf. Ovid *Tristia* 1.2.79–80, Statius *Silvae* 5.5.66–69, Martial 4.42.3–4).

5   **decus et dolor** The alliteration underscores the elegantly paradoxical phrase, which concisely expresses the notion that the deceased adorned the stages of Rome with his presence and was a source of distress when he died.

6   **omnes Veneres Cupidinesque** perhaps a proverbial phrase; cf. Catullus 3.1 (*lugete, o Veneres Cupidinesque*) and 13.12 (*donarunt Veneres Cupidinesque*). Cupid (Greek Eros) could sometimes be represented as a plurality of winged boys or young men; presumably the pl. *Veneres* arose by analogy. Here the implication may be that the deceased was especially skilled at acting scenes with erotic subject matter.

7   **sunt condita** When a compound subject consists of nouns of varying gender, modifiers either agree in gender with the noun closest to them or, as here, are neuter. The notion that when an outstanding artist has died, all the relevant arts (or even—in a striking hyperbole—some relevant divinities) are dead and buried with him, is found in other Latin epitaphs, including two composed for the poets Naevius and Plautus.

quo Paris understand *conditus est*; the antecedent of the rel. is *sepulchro*. Only now do we learn the name of the deceased. Paris was a popular actor of the pantomime, a dramatic genre in which, unlike the mime but like other forms of drama, the actors wore masks, male performers played female roles, there was singing and dancing, and the themes were often mythological. Paris was murdered on Domitian's orders in 82 or 83 CE after having been accused of an affair with the emperor's wife. It is probably not coincidental that Martial published this poem in a collection that appeared about thirteen years later, after Domitian's death.

11.14

1   **heredes** One of the duties that might come with being named someone's heir was that of providing for his or her burial. The statement that the heirs should *not* bury this man, and thus abandon his body to the worst of fates, is a paradox typical of Martial's poetry, creating the expectation of an explanation. Note the continuation of theme from the preceding poem, with a shift in tone from the serious to the parodic.

2   **quantulacumque** modifies *terra* ("even a tiny amount of earth")

   gravis predicate adj. with *est*, in its physical sense ("heavy"). Martial plays with a respectful formula found in many extant epitaphs: *sit tibi terra levis*, expressing a wish that the deceased may rest in peace, not disturbed by the weight of the earth above him or her. For jokes about physical appearance (in this case height) cf. 2.11.4, 3.43, 12.23.

11.15

   METER: Phalaecian hendecasyllable

1   **chartae** a metonymy for poems or collections of poems. In fact, the majority of Martial's epigrams avoid verbal obscenity, and Books 5 and 8 advertise themselves as being perfectly suitable reading for married ladies and children.

   Catonis uxor In a typical structure that creates a degree of syntactic suspense, the verb of which this is the subject comes in the following line. Both Cato the Censor and his great-grandson Cato the Younger were married twice, but rather than specifically referring to any of these women, Martial's phrase may be a generic evocation of the ideal austerity and chastity of the Roman matron.

2   **horribiles . . . Sabinae** The Sabines were a people of central
    Italy seen by Romans as rustic and unsophisticated, even rough
    (hence *horribiles*, a two-edged compliment at best, especially
    when applied to women), but their women were stereotypically
    chaste. "Cato's wife" and "Sabine women" thus stand for the
    kind of reader who might be shocked by blunt or obscene po-
    etry. The epigram following this one imagines Lucretia—the
    patron saint of womanly modesty among Romans—blushing
    and putting aside Martial's book in the presence of her hus-
    band Brutus, but picking it up again once her husband is gone
    (11.16.9–10: *erubuit posuitque meum Lucretia librum, / sed co-
    ram Bruto; Brute, recede: leget.*)

3   **hic . . . libellus** i.e., Book 11 in particular. The second poem of
    this book had announced that it was published to mark the Sat-
    urnalia (for which see on line 12 below).

    volo rideat i.e., *volo ut rideat,* a common ellipsis. This is the first
    in a series of clauses personifying Martial's book as a Roman
    man having fun at the Saturnalia.

4   **nequior** cf. 1.109.1

    libellis The technique of repeating a word from the end of the
    preceding line, but in a different case, is particularly character-
    istic of Catullus and Martial.

6   **pingui sordidus esse Cosmiano** The infinitive is complemen-
    tary with *erubescat* ("let him not be embarrassed to be . . .").
    Cosmus was a famous maker of perfumes and unguents, tradi-
    tionally used by Roman men and women at banquets and par-
    ties. The adj. *pingui* alludes to the fact that they were oil-based,
    but, like *sordidus* (and *horribiles* in line 2), comes with a certain
    ambivalence. The implication may be that the personified book
    overdoes the partying.

7   **ludat cum pueris, amet puellas** The combination of parallelism
    and variation is typical of Martial: the line is structured around
    two jussive subjunctives, one ending in *-at*, the other in *-et*, one
    intransitive and followed by *cum* + abl., the other transitive
    and followed by an acc. object. Since the verb *ludere* can have a

distinctly erotic charge (cf. colloquial English "fool around"), the two halves of this line suggest a stance typical of the Roman male persona: he enjoys the pleasures of eros with young people of both sexes. In the opening poem of his *Amores,* Ovid describes the appropriate subject matter of erotic verse as *aut puer aut longas compta puella comas* (*Amores* 1.1.20).

8   **per circuitus** i.e., through periphrasis or circumlocution, something the next line does quite skillfully

    illam The referent becomes clear two lines later; once again, syntactic suspense is created

10   **sanctus Numa** Numa Pompilius, the second king of Rome, was associated with the foundation of various religious institutions and known for his strength of character. The juxtaposition of his name with *mentulam* makes the use of that word—the Latin obscenity *par excellence*—all the more striking and underscores Martial's point: even the revered king Numa called a *mentula* a *mentula.*

12   **Saturnalicios** The Saturnalia, an annual holiday marking the winter solstice in December, was renowned for its carnivalesque atmosphere of festivities, drunkenness and gambling, frank speech, and temporary social reversals: slaves could order their masters around and were exempt from punishment, while citizens wore the *pilleum,* a cap that was the traditional symbol of freed slaves.

    Apollinaris perhaps Lucius Domitius Apollinaris, suffect consul in 97 CE, the year after this book was published, and also an acquaintance of Pliny the Younger. For those who recognize the name, this is a reminder that Martial has some highly placed acquaintances.

13   In other words: do not draw any conclusions about my character from what you read in my verse—especially verse composed for the Saturnalia! In making this distinction, Martial takes a stance adopted by other poets before him (cf. Catullus 16, Ovid *Tristia* 1.9.59–60, 2.353–56, 3.2.5–6).

11.70

1   **centenis milibus** understand *sestertium* (cf. 2.44.7); abl. of price with *emptos*. Note the use of the distributive: these slaves cost 100,000 sesterces *each*, a high price.

2   **plorantis dominos vendere** The image of young male slaves weeping as they face the prospect of being sold off is made all the more vivid by the oxymoronic juxtaposition *dominos vendere*. By describing these slaves as Tucca's *domini,* Martial evokes the complexities of power in erotic relations: in Tucca's affairs with his slaves, who wields what kind of power? Cf. 12.66.8 (*stant pueri dominos quos precer esse meos*) and consider the figure of the "mistress" in elegiac poetry, called both *puella* and *domina.*

    vendere, Tucca, potes Framing a couplet by repeating the same phrase is a technique particularly characteristic of Ovid and Martial.

3   **nec te blanditiae** The verb is suspended until the end of this couplet, whose evocation of the dynamics of Tucca's relationships with his slaves is as succinct as it is effective.

    verba perhaps something like "sweet nothings"; cf. Ovid *Amores* 2.19.17: *quas mihi blanditias, quam dulcia verba parabat.*

    rudes suggesting the slaves' youthful inexperience

4   **saucia colla** understand *eorum.* The imagery of wounding and warfare describes erotic passion throughout Latin literature (cf. Vergil *Aeneid* 4.1: *at regina gravi iamdudum saucia cura*) but in this instance there is also a concrete reference to love-bites or hickeys, a common theme in Latin erotic verse.

6   **tua mentula facta manu** The meter makes clear which noun is modified by *tua.* Tucca helped mold their bodies into maturity (the notion that sexual stimulation speeds up puberty seems to have been widespread).

7   **numerata** understand *tibi*: "counted out (i.e., paid) to you"

8   Lists and accumulations are characteristic techniques of Martial's epigrams; this one progresses from single objects to entire properties, both in the countryside and in the city. Tables (*mensas*) could

be quite expensive, particularly those made of citrus-wood from Africa. Vases called *murrina*, probably made of fluorspar and treated with myrrh resin, were known for their fragility and cost.

9 **vende senes servos** Comprare Cato the Elder's infamous advice to sell off old or sick slaves or animals (Cato, *De agr.* 2.7: *boves vetulos, armenta delicula, oves deliculas, lanam, pelles, plostrum vetus, ferramenta vetera, servum senem, servum morbosum, et si quid aliud supersit, vendat. patrem familias vendacem, non emacem esse oportet.*)

ignoscent Note the ironic exaggeration: everyone would understand your desire to keep these beautiful young slaves at any cost—even the old slaves you might need to sell off!

paternos i.e., slaves you have inherited from your father

11 **luxuria est emere hos** i.e., it is extravagant to pay so much for slaves.

12 **vendere luxuria est** Approaching paradox: because of their inestimable value, it would be extravagant to *sell* these slaves. Note that the final couplet, like the first, is framed by a repetition (*luxuria est ~ luxuria est*), the entire poem by references to selling (*vendere, Tucca, potes ~ vendere luxuria est*).

11.77

METER: iambic trimeter: ×– ∪– / ×– ∪– / ×– ∪–

One of the basic meters of dialogue scenes in Greek and Latin drama, the iambic trimeter is used in only one other epigram of Martial's (6.12) but is hardly unprecedented in the genre.

1 **Vacerra** a significant name (cf. 1.110.1) since *vacerra* means "log, stock, post" and could be an insult meaning "crazy, insane" (according to Suetonius *Augustus* 87.2, Augustus used the adj. *vacerrosus* in this sense)

quod introducing a noun clause ("[as for the fact] that . . ."), a quick and effective way of setting up a scenario that will just as quickly receive commentary in the epigram's third and final line

Fig. 5. A public latrine in Ostia. Photograph by AlMare / Wikimedia Commons.

conclavibus "the rooms," a euphemism for public toilets, which were a standard feature of Roman cities and remains of which survive in Pompeii, Ostia, Rome, and elsewhere. These were designed as communal spaces—rather than enclosed stalls, there were rows of seats with no dividers between them—and this and other texts confirm that they could be the site of social interactions.

3 **cenaturit** The verb is not found elsewhere in extant texts. Martial may or may not have coined it, but the desiderative suffix (cf. *es-urio,* "I want to eat, I am hungry") makes its meaning clear. Vacerra, in short, is comparable to Selius in Book 2: desperate for dinner invitations and not ashamed to do what it takes to obtain them.

cacaturit Martial clearly did not coin this verb, since it occurs in a graffito carved in a wall of the private latrine in a house in Pompeii (*Corpus Inscriptionum Latinarum* 4.5242, Casa del Centenario). Note how the final line of this brief epigram is thus framed by two rhyming verbs referring to complementary bodily functions.

∽ *Book 12*

12.3

1 **quod** understand *id* as antecedent: the syntactic function of the clause becomes clear in the following couplet

  Flacco Varioque . . . summoque Maroni Horace, Varius, and Vergil were among the Augustan poets supported by Maecenas (cf. 8.55, and for the use of their cognomina cf. 8.55.3)

2 **atavis regibus ortus eques** echoing the opening line of Horace's *Odes* 1.1 (*Maecenas atavis edite regibus*) but recasting it to fit a different meter and adding a reference to Maecenas' equestrian status

3 **gentibus et populis** dat. with *dicet* in the following line; the combination of nouns expresses the idea "the whole world"

  hoc referring back to *quod*

  te in apposition to *hoc*, both of them dependent on *fuisse* in the next line ("that you were this to me")

  Prisce Terenti cf. 8.12. Roman men might be identified by various combinations of their praenomen, nomen, and cognomen to differing effects. Praenomen alone (*Marce*) was the most intimate, praenomen + nomen (*Marce Tulli*) highly formal, nomen + cognomen (here, as not infrequently occurs, in reverse order) somewhere in between.

4 **fama . . . loquax chartaque . . . anus** compound subject of *dicet;* the verb, as often, agrees in number with the noun to which it is closest. The reference is to word of mouth and Martial's own poetry, written down on papyrus scrolls that will last.

5 **tu . . . tu . . . tu . . .** tricolon crescendo; the tone is elevated and respectful, almost hymnic

  tu, si quid posse videmur understand *facis* again after *tu*; for the pl. *videmur* cf. 1.35.13. In other words: it is because of you that I have my reputation for poetic ability, if I have one at all—an elegant formulation combining flattery of Terentius Priscus with a stance of humility.

6   You give me the privilege (*ius*) of indulging in the idleness (*pigritiae*) available to free-born Romans (*ingenuae*) by devoting my life to poetry.

7   **macte animi . . . morumque tuorum** The phrase *macte* (*esto*) ("be blessed for your . . ." or "hurrah for your . . .") may take either the gen. or the abl. Lines 7–12 of this epigram occur as the final lines of poem 12.6 in family β and Lindsay's Oxford Classical Text; the text as given here is found in manuscripts of family γ and printed by Shackleton Bailey in his Teubner edition.

8   **Numa** cf. 11.15.10

    hilaris . . . Cato Since neither Cato the Censor nor his great-grandson was known for a sense of humor, the point seems to be that the addressee has the upright character of a Cato without the grim severity.

9   **largiri, praestare . . . extendere . . . /et dare** The syntax of these infinitives will become clear in what follows.

    breves extendere census i.e., to give men gifts that increase their fortune. Pliny and others refer to the practice of enabling friends or dependents to qualify for the equestrian order by giving them gifts that raise their assessed worth (*census*) to the necessary 400,000 sesterces.

10 **quae** understand *ea* (acc. pl.) as antecedent

    faciles "generous"

11 **sed tu** introduces a contrast with *nunc* at the beginning of the line, and the generality of *licet* contrasts with the specificity of *tu*. Whereas this kind of generosity is now possible as a general principle, Priscus personally experienced a very different atmosphere under the previous emperor.

    sub principe duro referring to Domitian, assassinated in 96 CE and succeeded by Nerva and after him Trajan, who was emperor at the time Martial published Book 12. It is interesting to observe the contrast between this allusion to Domitian and Martial's references to the same emperor while he was alive (cf. 1.6, 6.1, 6.34, 7.5).

12.20

Meter: Phalaecian hendecasyllable

1　**quaeris** question-and-answer format (cf. 8.12.1)

2　**Themison** m. nom. sing. of a Greek name

habet sororem As often, Martial adopts the persona of the gossipmonger. His comment on Themison is made even more pointed by a double entendre: *soror* and *frater* were terms of endearment used by lovers, and the verb *habere* could mean "to posess sexually" (compare the similar play on words at Ovid *Metamorphoses* 9.497: *di nempe suas habuere sorores*). Nasty insinuations or gleeful accusations of incestuous relationships—brother-sister (e.g., Cicero's speech *Pro Caelio* on Clodius and Clodia), mother-son (e.g., Tacitus' *Annales* on Agrippina and Nero) and other combinations—are found in a number of Latin texts.

12.23

1　**dentibus atque comis ... emptis** cf. 1.72 for false teeth and wigs

2　**facies** from the verb *facio*, not the noun *facies*

oculo Problems with eyes were a standard target of physical humor among Romans, as the adjs. *lippus* (having watery or inflamed eyes, bleary-eyed) and *luscus* (having the use of only one eye) remind us.

non emitur in English idiom, "it *can't be* bought" or "you *can't* buy one"; for the Latin usage cf. Italian *non si compra*

12.68

1　**matutine cliens** i.e., a client who shows up at his patron's doorstep early in the morning for the *salutatio* (cf. 2.18). The word *cliens* has a certain bluntness: as opposed to the more courteous language of *amicitia*, the terms *patronus* and *cliens* openly point to the hierarchy and dependency implicit in patronage.

urbis mihi causa relictae The phrase is in apposition to *cliens*; as usual, *urbis* refers specifically to Rome; *mihi* is to be taken with *causa* ("the reason for me" = "my reason"). For the use of the pf. pass. pple. ("the city having been abandoned" = "the abandonment of the city"), cf. the title of Livy's history of Rome, *Ab urbe condita*. This epigram has a strongly autobiographical character: Martial had indeed left Rome for his native Spain, and at the time of the publication of Book 12 was a successful and well-known poet, about sixty years old. All the more significant, then, is the fact that he here places himself in the role of a patron complaining about annoying *clientes*, since he more often speaks in the voice of a client complaining about a demanding or ungrateful patron. This is typical of the varying perspectives adopted in Martial's epigrams, but also reminds us of the fluid nature of the Roman patronage system: one and the same man might simultaneously play the role of *cliens* to someone higher up on the social scale and that of *patronus* to an inferior.

2 **atria . . . ambitiosa** transferred epithet, i.e., the homes of wealthier and more powerful men than myself

3 **non sum ego causidicus** The scenario being sketched here is of a client coming to Martial for support or assistance in some legal matter. Contrast 8.17, where the speaker is precisely a *causidicus*.

4 **Pieridumque** The Muses could be called *Pierides* because they were said to have been born in Pieria in northern Greece.

5 **quae** the antecedent is *otia somnusque*

magna modifies *Roma*

6 **redeo** understand *Romam*; the colloquial usage of the pres. for the fut. in expressions like this is common in many languages. In other words: if even here in Spain I cannot sleep as late as I want because of *salutationes* and the like, I might as well return to Rome, where at least I can enjoy the advantages of the big city.

12.90

1   **pro sene ... amico** Experienced readers of Martial may become suspicious when they read of an old man—especially an old man in poor health—as someone's friend: cf. 1.10.4.

    sed clare "and with a loud voice at that" (presumably to make certain that people knew he was doing it)

    votum ... fecit The phrase refers to the practice of making a promise or vow to a god: if you grant me X, I will give you Y (e.g., an animal sacrifice, a statue or other object for the sanctuary, or a contribution of money). Thus *votum* is often translatable as "prayer."

    Maro a reminder that the referent of personal names sometimes only becomes clear from the context: this is hardly referring to Vergil (cf. 8.55.3)!

2   **cui** the antecedent is *sene amico*

3   **si ... non esset missus** the condition Maro places on his vow. The plpf. subjunctive emphasizes that the situation imagined in the protasis is logically prior to that of the apodosis, and the entire scenario takes place in the past (he vowed that, if the old man did not die first, he would subsequently ...).

    Stygias ... missus ad umbras cf. 1.93.2 for some other poetic phrases referring to death

4   **ut caderet ... victima** noun clause describing the substance of Maro's promise: "that a sacrificial animal would fall" (i.e., be killed at the altar)

5   **coeperunt** The lack of connective, somewhat unusual for narrative sequences such as this, underscores how surprising the turn of events is.

    certam ... spondere salutem i.e., they are confident he will recover

6   **ne votum solvat** The phrase describes the releasing of one's obligation to the god by giving the gift or making the promised sacrifice because one's request has been granted. The final verse is thus wryly paradoxical: Maro now prays that his prayers not be fulfilled.

12.91

METER: Phalaecian hendecasyllable

1   **communis tibi cum viro** "shared by your husband and you"

2   **exoletus** pf. pass. pple. of *exolesco*; when used of people, implicitly contrasted with *adolescens*. As a masculine substantive, the term refers to a prostitute who has passed the ideal period of youthful beauty. This epigram and a number of other ancient texts make it clear that male prostitutes were hired by both men and women.

3   **quare ... non sit** indirect question dependent upon *dic*, which is the main verb of this sentence

     minister a term for a slave, particularly in his capacity as server of food and drink

4   **times lagonam** i.e., you are afraid of what your husband might have the slave put in your wine. Anxious jokes and serious accusations deriving from the fear that spouses might try to kill one another were part of the urban landscape of Martial's Rome (cf. 9.15).

12.92

1   **Prisce** This may or may not refer to Terentius Priscus (cf. 8.12, 12.3).

2   **si fiam** Note the implications of this conditional sentence for Martial's persona: he represents himself as neither extremely wealthy nor particularly powerful. Such terms are of course relative. Martial consistently portrays himself as owning slaves and a country estate outside of Rome, as enjoying the friendship and support of a number of highly placed men, and as having been awarded the *ius trium liberorum* by two emperors (2.91–92).

3   **mores ... futuros** The implication is that if one's economic and social circumstances change, one's behavior and character (*mores*) will probably change with them.

4   **qualis eris** "what will you be like?" The combination of fut. less vivid protasis and fut. more vivid apodosis is hardly unusual.

12.93

METER: Phalaecian hendecasyllable

1   **qua . . . ratione** "a way in which she might . . .," "a way to . . .";
   equivalent to *quomodo*

   moechum cf. 7.10.13; equivalent to *adulterum*

2   **coram coniuge** The risks and challenges of carrying out an
   adulterous affair (especially in the presence of one's own spouse
   or the spouse of one's lover) are explored in a number of Martial's epigrams as well as a range of Latin poets, from Catullus to
   Ovid to Juvenal.

3   **morionem** The term (lit., "idiot, fool") here and elsewhere refers
   to a slave who functions as an entertainer at parties or banquets.

4   **multis . . . osculis** modifies *madentem*

5   **suis** understand *osculis* from the previous line

6   **dominae** Like English "mistress," the term is appropriately ambivalent here, since it casts the woman both as the slave's owner
   and as the man's lover.

7   **quanto** abl. of degree of difference with *maior*. Note the emphatic alliterations of this final line, delivering the pointed comment on the scenario just described.

   morio The final vowel is shortened (cf. 1.24.4).

❧ *Book 13*

13.3

1   **gracili** For the aesthetic of the thin and slender, cf. 1.1.3.

   Xeniorum dependent upon *turba*. The Greek title of this book
   refers to gifts given to guests (*xenoi*) to take home with them.
   Martial's couplets are designed to accompany such gifts and
   seem to have been written for the Saturnalia, for which cf. 11.15.

2   **constabit . . . tibi** In this sense ("to be available for the price of"),
   the Latin verb *constare* is the source of Italian *costare*, French
   coûter, and English *cost*.

   nummis cf. 8.17.2; abl. of price (not an especially high price)

4   **et faciat lucrum** "and he would still make a profit"

Tryphon For Martial's references to booksellers and their shops, cf. 1.2. Tryphon was evidently an important bookseller: Quintilian's *Institutio Oratoria* opens with a letter addressed to him.

5   **licet . . . mittas** i.e., *licet ut mittas* (cf. 2.23.1, 8.55.12); best translated not "it is permitted for you to send" or "you are allowed to send," but "you can/may send."

hospitibus As is also true of Italian *ospite*, the term refers to both parties in an act of hospitality, distinguished in English as "guest" and "host." Linguistic or cultural context will usually make the meaning clear.

pro munere "as a gift," i.e., instead of the object itself

7   **titulos** the headings or brief titles that are placed above each couplet in the manuscripts

rebus dat. pl. with *addita*, referring to the items described in the couplets

8   **praetereas** jussive subjunctive expressing an imperative (cf. 1.15.6). Martial elsewhere makes comparable suggestions for how to read his poetry.

non facit ad stomachum "is not to your taste." The idiomatic metaphor is particularly apt here, since most of the gifts described in the *Xenia* are food items.

13.4

tus Incense was, among other things, burned as an offering to cult statues.

1   **serus** A traditional wish for the emperor found as early as Augustan poetry was this: May much time pass before you reach your heavenly home (cf. Horace *Odes* 1.2.45).

Germanicus the agnomen adopted by Domitian after a military victory over the Chatti; cf. 9.5

2   **utque diu terris** understand *imperet* again

da The imperative is addressed to the anonymous recipient of this couplet and/or of the gift that it notionally accompanies.

13.14

1   The word order of this verse is fairly elaborate but not unusual in Latin poetry: the rel. clause **cludere quae cenas . . . solebat avorum** (with postponed rel. pron.) is interrupted by its antecedent (*lactuca*), and the gen. *avorum* is noticeably separated from the noun on which it depends (*cenas*).

2   **nostras** contrasted with *avorum*. The contrast between today's practices and those of the ancestors, almost always to the detriment of the former, is a commonplace in Latin literature (cf. 5.81, but see also 8.55). The change in dining practice to which Martial refers seems to have occurred after the time of Augustus and may have been justified by a belief that lettuce and wine were incompatible (the heaviest drinking of wine typically occurred at the end of the dinner), or by the belief that lettuce had both appetite-inducing and laxative properties: loosening one's bowels at the beginning of a long meal might aid digestion. In all its humor and seeming triviality, the epigram asks a pointed question with broader cultural implications: Why have we reversed the way things used to be done?

inchoat This is the reading of family α; manuscripts of families β and γ have the subjunctive *inchoet*. The editorial choice is difficult, since either a direct question (*dic mihi: cur inchoat?*) or an indirect question (*dic mihi cur inchoet*) would be possible.

illa referring back to *lactuca* in the previous line

13.29

Damascenorum damsons or Damascus prunes, inexpensive Saturnalian gifts

1   **peregrinae carie rugosa senectae** a humorously elaborate turn of phrase: they have withered in an aging process that took place outside of their native land

2   **duri solvere ventris onus** i.e., they have a laxative effect; cf. 1.37 for the language

13.63

1 **nimis** modifies *macresceret*

exhausto . . . inguine Since *inguen* is a common euphemism for the genitals (cf. English "groin"), the phrase refers to sexual over-exertion—which according to a Roman belief could cause males of all species, including humans, to be come unappealingly skinny.

gallus in the sense "rooster"

2 **amisit** perhaps ironic: he "lost" his testicles to castration the way one might "lose" someone to death (cf. 1.33.1, 7.14.2)

mihi ethical dat.: to my mind, as far as I am concerned, as I see things

gallus The repetition of the noun from the end of the preceding line introduces an untranslatable pun on two senses of the word: "rooster" and "castrated priest of Cybele" (cf. 1.35, 10.4, 14.204). English translations often use a different but equally effective pun: "Now I will consider him—a cock!" (T. J. Leary), "Now I shall consider him—a cockerel!" (D. R. Shackleton Bailey).

13.74

1 **haec** modifies *avis*

Tarpei scans *Tar-pē-ī*

templa poetic pl. The allusion is to a famous incident during the Gauls' attack on Rome in 390 BCE. When the enemy stealthily entered the city at night, a flock of geese sacred to Juno kept on the Capitoline Hill were startled awake and alarmed the sleeping Romans with their cries, thus saving the city and its temples. The most prominent and symbolically potent of the various temples on the Capitoline was that of Jupiter Optimus Maximus Capitolinus, one of the epithets of Jupiter (the Roman version of the Indo-European sky god) was *Tonans*, and the Capitoline hill was also called *Mons Tarpeius*.

2 **illa** i.e., *templa*

deus i.e., Domitian, who after a destructive fire had lavishly restored the Capitoline temple, rededicating it in 82 CE. The point is that thanks to Domitian's intervention the temple is now safe from destruction, and the addressee is imagined as being surprised (*miraris*) that it could ever have been otherwise.

13.82

1   **ebria . . . veni** Following a long tradition in epigrammatic poetry, an object is personified and speaks up. The oyster describes itself as "drunk" because it has soaked in the waters of the Lucrine Lake near the resort town of Baiae on the Bay of Naples, renowned for the quality of its oyster farms. There may also be an allusion to Baiae's reputation for drunken excess.

2   **luxuriosa** The personification continues: the oyster is not only drunk but has expensive tastes. Only the best sauce will suit her.

  garum a fundamental element in Roman cooking, a salty fermented fish sauce that came in a wide range of varieties and qualities. Martial may be alluding to the renowned variety produced in Pompeii, also in the Bay of Naples region (Pliny *Naturalis Historia* 31.94).

13.108

  mulsum mead or honeyed wine; the most prized variety was made from Falernian wine and Attic honey

1   **Attica . . . mella** cf. 6.34.4. Again the object is personified, but instead of speaking up as in 13.82, it is addressed in the second person

  nectareum . . . Falernum cf. 8.55.14. The adj. suggests that the wine is fit for the gods to drink, and perhaps also that it is of the sweet variety (Pliny *Naturalis Historia* 14.63 identifies three types of Falernian: *austerum, dulce, tenue*). The arrangement of the verse suggests the process of mingling: not only is it a "golden line" (abVAB: cf. spect.1.7) but it displays a chiastic ABCBA arrangement (place - substance - mixing - substance - place).

  turbatis "cloud" and perhaps also "disturb"

2   **Ganymede** cf. 1.6. The reference to Ganymede picks up on the implications of *nectareum*: no mere mortals should be mixing honey—not even Attic honey—into this outstanding wine.

❧ *Book 14*

14.73

1   **psittacus** Parrots and other birds who imitate human speech were quite popular among Romans, the subject of a number of anecdotes, jokes and poems (cf. Ovid *Amores* 2.6 and Statius *Silvae* 2.4). The poem opening Book 14 indicates that its epigrams will alternate between expensive and simple gifts (14.1.5: *divitis alternas et pauperis accipe sortes*); the parrot is an expensive gift.

  discam That inanimate objects can be personified and even speak is an established tradition in Greek and Latin epigrammatic poetry, but in this case the technique has a witty edge, since the epigram is in the voice of a bird who is describing his ability to imitate human speech.

2   **hoc** referring forward to what follows, and contrasted with *aliorum nomina* in the previous line

  per me "by myself," contrasted with *a vobis* in the preceding line, as the tense of *didici* is contrasted with that of *discam*. The intertwined themes of this couplet—birds who salute the emperor by name, and the emperor's quasi-divine power over animals—are found in other ancient texts as well (cf. Pliny *Naturalis Historia* 10.117, Statius *Silvae* 2.4, Martial spect.17, 1.104).

14.134

  fascia pectoralis the Roman predecessor of the modern brassiere, a band of cloth tied around the chest to hold the breasts; an inexpensive gift

1   **fascia** vocative sing.: again the object is addressed

crescentes This probably implies that the gift is meant for an adolescent whose breasts are just beginning to grow, but Leary sees a reference to an adult woman who is putting on weight.

dominae the future "mistress" or "owner" of the breast-band and/or the speaker's "mistress"

compesce "keep in place" and perhaps also "prevent from growing further"

papillas The noun literally refers to the nipple, whether of a male or of a female, but in a common synecdoche can refer to the entire breast (cf. *culus*, literally denoting the anus, but often referring to the buttocks).

2   **ut sit** purpose clause

quod capiat . . . tegatque rel. clause of characteristic: "something for my hand to hold and cover." Martial here and elsewhere appeals to an apparently widespread aesthetic of breasts small enough to be covered by a single hand (cf. 2.56, a joke about a woman with excessively large breasts).

14.188

1   **comes . . . tibi fuerit** "will be your companion," "will accompany you." The fut. pf. refers to an action prior to that of the main verb, the fut. imperative *putato*: if you bring this book along with you, you ought (subsequently) to think of it this way.

membrana cf. 1.2.3; codex editions made of parchment were expensive

2   **carpere . . . vias** "to take journeys." Martial elsewhere describes a compact edition of his own works in similar terms (1.2.2, *et comites longae quaeris habere viae*). Taking books on long trips was evidently a common practice among upper-class Romans.

cum Cicerone playing with the common metonymy whereby a poet's name stands for his work (cf. 1.2.4). If you take "Cicero" (i.e., a selection of Cicero's works) along with you, you can imagine that Cicero himself is with you.

14.189

Monobiblos Propertius' poetry has been handed down in four books. Martial apparently uses *Monobiblos* to refer to Book 1, dominated by the figure of Cynthia, and many modern scholars do likewise. Whether Propertius himself did is debatable.

1   **Cynthia** In another metonymy (cf. *cum Cicerone*, 14.188.2), the name of Propertius' lover also functions as the title of the book of poetry in which she so prominently figures and which she opens with her name: *Cynthia prima suis miserum me cepit ocellis* (Propertius 1.1.1).

    carmen in apposition to *Cynthia*; somewhat unusually referring not an individual poem but to a collection of poems ("Propertius' poetry")

2   **dedit** understand *famam* again. The line is framed by two verbs of opposed meaning (*accepit . . . dedit*), underscoring the way in which poetry can be two-way street. Cynthia (both the character and the poetry she dominates) became famous and made Propertius famous in turn.

14.190

1   **pellibus** A variation on *membranis* in the title, the word refers to parchment made from the skin of goats or sheep, more durable and more costly than papyrus

    exiguis contrasted with *ingens*; a massive work fits into a slim volume

    artatur either "is abridged" (referring to a selection of excerpts or an epitome of Livy's work) or "is confined," i.e., within the covers of a codex edition containing his complete works in miniature format. Pliny *Naturalis Historia* 7.85 refers to a text of the *Iliad* written in a walnut shell!

    Livius ingens Livy's *Ab urbe condita,* a history of Rome from its foundation to his own day, consisted of 142 books, of which only Books 1–10 and 21–45 survive more or less intact.

2   **non totum** It would indeed be difficult, though not impossible, for a home library to hold all of Livy's works in the usual format

of one papyrus scroll per book. The so-called Villa dei Papiri at Herculaneum had a large home library, thought by many to be based on the philosopher Philodemus' personal collection and consisting of well over a thousand scrolls.

14.191

1   **hic erit** Either *hic* is the adv. and *tibi* is implied ("here [i.e., accompanying this epigram] you will find Sallust, who in the judgment of scholars is first") or else *hic* is the demonstrative (cf. 1.1.1) and *primus* the predicate: "this man, in the judgment of scholars, will be the first," i.e., will never be surpassed.

    ut perhibent doctorum corda virorum for this meaning of *cor,* cf. 3.27.4. Many Roman writers had a high opinion of Sallust: Quintilian (*Institutio Oratoria* 10.1.101) compares him to Thucydides, and Tacitus (*Annales* 3.30.1) calls him *rerum Romanarum florentissimus auctor.*

2   **Romana . . . in historia** i.e., in the writing of Roman history. Of Sallust's writings, only the *Catilina* and *Jugurtha* survive intact, but he also wrote five books of *Historiae.*

    Crispus cf. 8.55.3 for the use of the cognomen alone

14.194

1   **quidam** Over the centuries Lucan's critics have included Quintilian (*Institutio Oratoria* 10.1.90: *magis oratoribus quam poetis imitandus*) and Servius (ad *Aen.* 1.382: *videtur historiam composuisse, non poema*). On the other hand, Aper in Tacitus' *Dialogus de oratoribus* (20.5) lists Lucan along with Horace and Vergil as excellent sources of the *poeticus decor* that an orator ought to strive for.

    non esse poetam The criticism has been made both because of his style, which some have considered more rhetorical than poetic, and because his epic poem on the civil war between Caesar and Pompey departs from established tradition by leaving the gods entirely out of the narrative.

2   **qui me vendit** As often, the rel. clause precedes its antecedent (*bibliopola*). For the poet-poetry metonymy and for booksellers in Martial's Rome, cf. 1.2 (e.g., 5: *ubi sim venalis*) and 13.3.

14.195

Catullus It is not clear whether this refers to a complete edition of Catullus or a selection, whether in the usual scroll or in the codex format.

1   **tantum . . . debet** Cities and towns around the Roman world could capitalize on their reputation for their famous authors. Perhaps inspired by Ovid *Amores* 3.15, Martial 1.61 offers a miniature catalogue—Mantua is known for Vergil; Padua for Livy, Stella, and Flaccus; and so on—to which he adds Bilbilis, known for Licinianus and himself!

   magna . . . Verona . . . / parva . . . Mantua Whereas Verona was a fairly important city, especially in post-Augustan times, Mantua is seldom mentioned in ancient texts apart from its association with Vergil, who was born in the nearby village of Andes.

2   Note the structure of the line, perfectly identical to that of the first verse except for the omitted verb. Each line thus ends with a juxtaposition of two proper names: first the city, then the poet.

14.198

1   **delicias** Here, unlike 1.109.5, this refers not to the dog herself ("pet") but to the delights she brings.

   parvae . . . catellae The sequence of epigrams shows that the dog qualifies as an inexpensive gift.

2   **brevis est pagina tota** i.e., an entire column or page (cf. 9 praef.) could not contain all that I want to say about her—let alone a single couplet. It is interesting to compare 1.109, a long epigram on the delights of a dog named Issa.

14.199

asturco a small horse from Asturia in northwestern Spain, an expensive gift (cf. Petronius *Satyricon* 86.6)

1 **brevis** Note the appearance of this adj. in the second line of the preceding poem. Here, referring to the horse, it means "small, tiny."

ad numeros "rhythmically, in time"; Pliny *Naturalis Historia* 8.166 refers to the manner of trotting peculiar to *asturcones*.

colligit "picks up, raises," i.e., trots

2 **auriferis gentibus** Asturia in particular and Spain in general were known for their gold.

14.200

canis vertragus an inexpensive gift. The word *vertragus* was a borrowing from a Celtic language and seems to mean "fast runner" (*trag-* is probably cognate with Greek *trekhō* and *ver-* is an intensifier). It clearly refers to a type of dog known for speed, but it is not certain which particular breed, if any, is meant.

1 **non sibi sed domino** dats. of advantage ("hunts for the benefit of . . ."). As with its equivalents in English and a number of other languages, the Latin word *dominus* can refer both to a slave's master and an animal's owner.

2 **inlaesum . . . dente** understand *suo*; abl. of means. The ability to retrieve game without damaging it has long been prized in hunting dogs.

14.203

puella Gaditana Gades in Spain (today Cadiz) was known for its tradition of training young women in an erotically stimulating dance, complete with castanets, cymbals, and suggestive gyrations. As this epigram makes clear, these dancers were often slaves; this is an expensive gift.

1 **tremulum . . . blandum** n. acc. sing., used adverbially

prurit Note that the verb is intransitive: the reference is not to her sexual stimulation of the audience but to her enactment of *being* stimulated.

2   **masturbatorem . . . Hippolytum** Best known from Euripides' play by the same name, this mythological figure was renowned for his chaste rejection of the advances of his stepmother Phaedra and of sexual experience in general. The image is thus humorously paradoxical, further emphasizing the dancer's abilities.

fecerit The pf. subjunctive follows the standard sequence of tenses in a result clause, but also has a contrafactual function: her techniques are so stimulating that, *if* she had performed for Hippolytus, she *would have had* this effect on him.

14.204

cymbala an inexpensive gift, thematically linked with the preceding gift, since dancers from Cadiz used both castanets and cymbals

1   **aera** *āē-ră,* acc. pl. of *āēs, āēris,* "bronze" (as opposed to *ā-ĕ-ră,* acc. sing. of *āēr, āĕris,* "air"). By a common metonymy, the noun refers to a bronze object, in this case a pair of cymbals (cf. *ferrum,* "iron" but also "sword").

Celaenaeos lugentia matris amores The beautiful young Attis came from Phrygia in Asia Minor, in some traditions from the city of *Celaenae.* Cybele, mother of the gods (*matris*) fell in love with him (here *amores,* as often when it is in the pl., refers to the beloved person). After Attis broke a vow of chastity, she drove him insane, whereupon he castrated himself and died. In both the textual and the visual tradition, the *galli*—who castrated themselves in emulation of Attis—are depicted with tambourines and cymbals, with which they honored Cybele and mourned for Attis; hence *lugentia.*

2   **esuriens** implying that, if he needs to buy some food, he will not hesitate to sell them off. See Apuleius *Metamorphoses* 8.24–31 for an unsympathetic portrayal of a group of *galli.*

14.205

puer an expensive gift. Note the sequence of 14.203–205: desirable female slave; cymbals belonging to *galli*, who are neither fully male nor female; desirable male slave.

1   **aetate . . . non pumice levis** abl. of means; note the distinction between *lēvis* and *lĕvis*. The wish being expressed is that the slave be young enough to be naturally smooth, not yet needing to resort to artificial means of depilation.

2   Note the sound effects of this verse, distributed between its two halves: *propter quem placeat // nulla puella mihi*. The alliteration continues a pattern from the preceding line: *puer, non pumice levis*.

nulla puella The Latin textual tradition is full of men's musings on the respective advantages of young men and women as sexual partners. Occasional assertions of a preference for one over the other do not invite being taken as absolute statements of a lifelong commitment. On the contrary, those few allusions to men whose sexual experience was strictly limited to one sex or the other suggest that such exclusivity was the exception that proved the rule.

Appendix A

∾ Map of the Mediterranean region

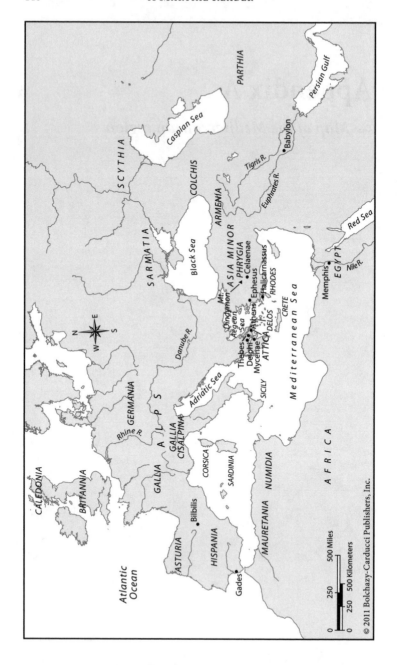

Appendix B

∾ Map of Italy

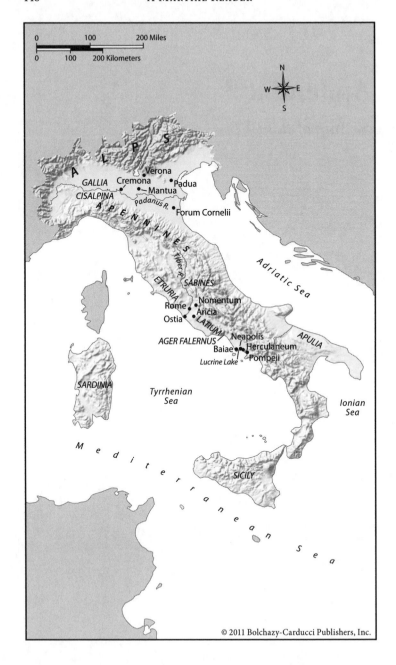

© 2011 Bolchazy-Carducci Publishers, Inc.

Vocabulary

ā *or* ab, *prep.* + *abl.*, from, away
from; by (*agent*)

abdūcō, -ere, -dūxī, -ductum,
to lead away, steal

abeō, -īre, -iī *or* -īvī, -itum, to
go away, leave, depart

abigō, -ere, -ēgī, -actum, to
drive away, remove, dispel

abscīdō, -ere, -cīdī, -cīsum, to
cut off, cut out

abscondō, -ere, -condī *or*
-condidī, -conditum, to
conceal, hide, keep secret

abstulerat. *See* auferō

accidit, -ere, -cidit, —, *impers.*,
it happens, occurs

accipiō, -ere, -cēpī, -ceptum, to
receive, take, acquire, accept

accumbō, -ere, -cubuī,
-cubitum, to lie down,
recline, take one's place at
table

ācer, ācris, ācre, *adj.*, sharp,
bright, vivid; vigorous,
energetic; severe, violent,
intense

acerbus, -a, -um, *adj.*, sour,
bitter; pitiless, cruel, harsh

ad, *prep.* + *acc.*, to, towards; for,
the purpose of

addō, -ere, -didī, -ditum, to
add, attach

adeō, -īre, -iī *or* -īvī, -itum, to
go toward, approach

adserō, -ere, -seruī, -sertum, to
lay claim to; defend, protect,
preserve

adsertor, -ōris, *m.*, defender,
protector, champion

adsiduus, -a, -um, *adj.*,
constantly present,
persistent, uninterrupted,
constant

adstō, -stāre, -stitī, —, to stand
by, stand at, stand on; stand
waiting, stand still

adsum, -esse, -fuī, —, to be
present, be here/there, attend

adulter, -erī, *m.*, adulter, lover
of a married woman

Aegaeus, -a, -um, *adj.*, of or
related to the Aegean Sea

aeger, -gra, -grum, *adj.*, ill,
sick; weary, exhausted;
distressed, troubled

Aeglē, -ēs, *f., proper name*, Aegle

Aemiliānus, -ī, *m., proper
name*, Aemilianus

āer, āeris (*acc.* āerem *or* āera),
m., air, atmosphere

aes, aeris, *n.*, bronze, copper, brass; coin; cash, money

aetās, -tātis, *f.*, lifetime, age, era

aetherius, -a, -um, related to the sky or the heavens, lofty

Aetia, -ōrum, *n. pl.*, "Causes, Origins" (*title of a poem by Callimachus*)

ager, agrī, *m.*, piece of land, tract, territory, field

agō, -ere, ēgī, actum, to drive, bring, carry; do, perform, achieve

āh *or* **ā**, *interjection expressing distress, regret, pity, surprise, etc.*

Alexis, -idis, *m., proper name*, Alexis

alica, -ae (*also* **halica, -ae**), *f.*, emmer groats, porridge; (*also* **hal[l]ec, hal[l]ēcis**, *n.*) a type of fish-sauce

aliter, *adv.*, otherwise, differently

alius, -a, -ud, *adj.*, different, another, other; **alius . . . alius**: one . . . another; **aliī . . . aliī**: some . . . others

alter, altera, alterum (*gen.* **alterīus**), *adj.*, a further, another, the other (of two)

amārus, -a, -um, *adj.*, bitter, pungent, harsh, caustic

amātrix, -trīcis, *f.*, (female) lover; (*as f. adj.*) loving, a lover's, amorous

ambitiōsus, -a, -um, anxious to win favor, eager for glory, ambitious; ostentatious

ambulātor, -ōris, *m.*, one who walks about or strolls

amīca, -ae, *f.*, (female) friend, girlfriend, lover

amīcus, -ī, *m.*, (male) friend, boyfriend, lover

āmittō, -ere, -mīsī, -missum, to send away, dismiss, release, let go, lose

amō (1), to love, feel affection for, be fond of

amor, -ōris, *m.*, love, affection, fondness; (*pl.*) beloved, darling

amphitheātrum, -ī, *n.*, an oval or circular theater, amphitheater

animus, -ī, *m.*, mind, spirit, attitude; disposition; courage, pride

annus, -ī, *m.*, year

anser, -eris, *m./f.*, goose

ante, *prep.* + *acc.*, in front of, before

anteambulō (1), to walk in front of

antequam, *conj.*, before

antīquus, -a, -um, *adj.*, ancient, old

anus, -ūs, *f.*, old woman; (*as f. adj.*) old, aged

anxius, -a, -um, *adj.*, worried, uneasy, anxious

apertus, -a, -um, *adj.*, open, free from obstacles, uncovered, exposed

apis, -is, *f.*, bee

Apollināris, -is, *m., proper name*, Apollinaris

aptus, -a, -um, *adj.,* tied, fastened; prepared, equipped, ready; suitable, apt

apud, *prep.* + *acc.,* at, toward, near; at the house of, in the country of; in the presence of

aqua, -ae, *f.,* water

aquila, -ae, *f.,* eagle

Aquīnus, -ī, *m., proper name,* Aquinus

āra, -ae, *f.,* altar

arca, -ae, *f.,* chest, coffer, box (*especially for keeping money*)

arcānus, -a, -um, *adj.,* secret, private, inmost, intimate

argentum, -ī, *n.,* silver, objects made of silver

Argīlētānus, -a, -um, *adj.,* pertaining to the Argiletum (*a street and district in Rome*)

argūtus, -a, -um, *adj.,* clear-sounding, clear-voiced, eloquent, clever

Arīcīnus, -a, -um, *adj.,* pertaining to Aricia (*a town in Latium*)

arma, -ōrum, *n. pl.,* weapons, arms, warfare

Armenius, -a, -um, *adj.,* Armenian, pertaining to Armenia

Arria, -iae, *f., proper name,* Arria

ars, artis, *f.,* skill, craft, technique; trick, craftiness; artifice, artistry, art

artō (1), to pull tight, restrict, reduce, compress

artus, -ūs, *m.,* a joint in the body; arm, leg; body part

as, assis, *m.,* a copper coin (*of small value*)

aspiciō, -ere, -spexī, -spectum, to look at, gaze upon, observe; perceive, consider

Assyrius, -a, -um, *adj.,* Assyrian

astrum, -ī, *n.,* star

Astur, -uris, *m.,* Asturian, inhabitant of Asturia (*region in Spain*)

asturcō, -ōnis, *m.,* an Asturian horse

at *or* **ast,** *conj.,* but, however, on the other hand

atavus, -ī, *m.,* great-great-great-grandfather; remote ancestor, forefather

atque *or* **ac,** *conj.,* and, too, and what is more

ātrium, -iī, *n.,* atrium (*central room in Roman house*)

attagēna, -ae, *f., a type of bird similar to the partridge*

Attica, -ae, *f.,* Attica (*region in central Greece where Athens is located*)

Attis, -idis, *m., proper name,* Attis

attonitus, -a, -um, *adj.,* thunderstruck, stunned, dazed

auctor, -ōris, *m.,* person responsible for something; originator, source; author

audeō, -ēre, ausus sum, to be bold, have the courage to, venture upon

audiō, -īre, -īvī, -ītum, to hear, listen

aula, -ae, *f.,* royal or noble residence, palace; royal or imperial household, court

Aulus, -ī, *m., proper name,* Aulus

aura, -ae, *f.,* breeze, wind

aurifer, -era, -erum, *adj.,* containing or yielding gold

auris, -is, *f.,* ear

aurum, -ī, *n.,* gold

aut, *conj.,* or, or else; **aut . . . aut,** either . . . or

avidus, -a, -um, *adj.,* greedy, voracious, insatiable

avis, -is, *f.,* bird; omen, portent

Avītus, -ī, *m., proper name,* Avitus

avus, -ī, *m.,* grandfather; ancestor, forefather

Babylōn, -ōnis *or* **-ōnos,** *f.,* Babylon (*ancient city on the Euphrates, capital of Babylonia*)

Bāiānus, -a, -um, *adj.,* pertaining to Baiae (*resort town on the Bay of Naples*)

barbarus, -a, -um, *adj.,* foreign, barbarian

bāsiātiō, -ōnis, *f.,* kiss

bāsiō (1), to kiss

bāsium, -iī, *n.,* kiss

Bassus, -ī, *m., proper name,* Bassus

beātus, -a, -um, *adj.,* happy, fortunate; rich, wealthy

bellum, -ī, *n.,* war, warfare

bene, *adv.,* well, efficiently, correctly, suitably, successfully

bibliopōla, -ae, *m.,* bookseller

bibliothēca, -ae, *f.,* collection of books, library (*both private and public*)

bibō, -ere, bibī, —, to drink

bis, *adv.,* twice

Bithӯnicus, -a, -um, *adj.,* pertaining to Bithynia (*region of Asia Minor*)

blandior, -īrī, -ītus sum, to behave or speak charming or ingratiatingly, flatter, fawn upon

blanditiae, -ārum, *f. pl.,* ingratiating behavior, flattery, blandishments, charm

blandus, -a, -um, *adj.,* charming, ingratiating, seductive; gentle, soft, pleasant

bōlētus, -ī, *m., a type of mushroom*

bonus, -a, -um, *adj.,* good, virtuous, satisfactory

brācchium, -iī, *n.,* forearm, arm

brevis, -e, *adj.,* brief, short

bucca, -ae, *f.,* lower part of cheek, mouth

cacāturiō, -īre, -iī, —, to want or need to shit

cacō (1), to shit

cadō, -ere, cecidī, cāsum, to fall, droop, drop; be killed, die (*especially in battle*)

Caeciliānus, -ī, *m., proper name,* Caecilianus

caedō, -ere, cecīdī, caesum, to strike, beat, kill, cut down

Caesar, -aris, *m., proper name,* Caesar

Caesareus, -a, -um, *adj.,* pertaining to Caesar or the emperor

caldus, -a, -um, *or* **calidus, -a, -um,** *adj.,* hot, warm

Calēdonia, -ae, *f.,* Caledonia *(region of northern Scotland)*

calīgō (1), to be dark or gloomy; have blurred vision, be blinded in judgment

callidus, -a, -um, *adj.,* expert, clever, ingenious, cunning

Callimachus, -ī, *m., proper name,* Callimachus

calvus, -a, -um, *adj.,* bald, having the head shaved

Camillus, -ī, *m., proper name,* Camillus

canis, -is, *m./f.,* dog, hound

cantō (1), sing, recite, tell of

cānus, -a, -um, *adj.,* white, white- or grey-haired, ancient

capillus, -ī, *m.,* hair *(of the head)*

capiō, -ere, cēpī, captum, take hold of, catch, get, obtain; captivate, charm; hold, contain

cāpō, -ōnis, *m.,* castrated rooster, capon

captō (1), to try to obtain, seek to catch, hunt for *(figuratively)*

caput, capitis, *n.,* head *(of a human being or animal),* upper or extreme part *(of things)*

Cār, Cāris, *m.,* a Carian, inhabitant of Caria *(in Asia Minor)*

carchēsium, -iī, *n., a type of drinking-cup*

cariēs, -iēī, *f.,* decay, rot

carmen, -inis, *n.,* solemn or ritual utterance; song; poem

carpō, -ere, carpsī, carptum, to pluck, gather, pick; pull pieces off; eat away, erode

cārus, -a, -um, *adj.,* expensive, costly; beloved, dear

castrō (1), to castrate

castus, -a, -um, *adj.,* chaste, pure

catella, -ae, *f.,* small female dog, puppy

catēnātus, -a, -um, *adj.,* in chains, secured by a chain; arranged in a chain or series

Catilīna, -ae, *m., proper name,* Catiline

Catō, -ōnis, *m., proper name,* Cato

Catullus, -ī, *m., proper name,* Catullus

causa, -ae, *f.,* legal case, trial; reason, excuse, pretext; reason, ground, cause

causidicus, -ī, *n.,* an advocate, pleader of legal cases

caveō, -ēre, cāvī, cautum, to take precautions; beware, guard against

Cecropius, -a, -um, *adj.,* pertaining to Cecrops (*first king of Attica*), Athenian

cēdō, -ere, cessī, cessum, to withdraw, step aside, make way for, yield to

Celaenaeus, -a, -um, *adj.,* pertaining to Celaenae (*town of Phrygia in Asia Minor*)

celer, celeris, celere, *adj.,* fast, speedy, quick

celsus, -a, -um, *adj.,* lofty, tall, high

cēna, -ae, *f.,* dinner, supper (*main meal of the day*)

cēnāturiō, -īre, —, —, to desire to have dinner

cēnō (1), to dine, have dinner

cēnsūra, -ae, *f.,* the office or powers of the censor; moral oversight or control

cēnsus, -ūs, *m.,* registration of citizens (*done every five years*); monetary qualification for a particular class; property, wealth

Centaurus, -ī, *m.,* Centaur (*mythic being, half-man and half-horse*)

centēnī, -ae, -a, *adj.,* one hundred each, groups of one hundred

centum, *indecl. adj.,* one hundred

certus, -a, -um, *adj.,* definite, certain, sure, assured

cērussātus, -a, -um, *adj.,* painted with white lead

charta, -ae *or* **carta, -ae,** *f.,* paper, writings on paper

Chionē, -ēs, *f., proper name,* Chione

Chloē, -ēs, *f., proper name,* Chloe

Cicerō, -ōnis, *m., proper name,* Cicero

cinaedus, -ī, *m., effeminate male dancer; insult for an effeminate man, especially one who plays the receptive role in anal intercourse*

cinctus, -a, -um, *adj.,* belted, surrounded, bordered, enclosed

cinis, cineris, *m.,* ashes, embers

circuitus, -ūs, *or* **circumitus, -ūs,** *m.,* circumference, perimeter; indirect route or method, detour

civīlis, -is, -e, *adj.,* pertaining to citizens; pertaining to civil war

clārus, -a, -um, *adj.,* loud, bright, clear; well-known, famous, illustrious

Claudia, -ae, *f., proper name,* Claudia

Claudius, -ī, *m., proper name,* Claudius

cliēns, -ntis, *m.,* man dependent upon a social superior, client

clīvus, -ī, *m.,* slope, incline

clūdō, -ere, clūsī, clūsum *or* **claudō, -ere, clausī, clausum,** to close, shut, conclude

coactus, -a, -um, *adj.* (*pf. pass. pple. of* **cōgō**), compressed, forced

cocus, -ī, *or* **coquus, -ī,** *m.,* cook

coepī, coepisse, coeptum, to begin, initiate

cognōscō, -ere, cognōvī, cognitum, to get to know, learn, find out, discern

Colchis, -idis *or* **-idos,** *f.,* woman from Colchis (*region to the east of the Black Sea*)

colligō, -ere, collēgī, collectum, to gather together, collect, accumulate

collum, -ī, *n.,* neck

colō, -ere, -uī, cultum, to inhabit, cultivate; adorn; worship; devote oneself to, court

colōnus, -ī, *m.,* farmer, tenant-farmer

colossus, -ī, *m.,* huge statue (*especially the famous statue of the sun-god at Rhodes*)

columba, -ae, *f.,* pigeon, dove

coma, -ae, *f.,* the hair of the head; foliage

comātus, -a, -um, *adj.,* having long hair

comes, comitis, *m./f.,* companion, comrade; follower, devotee

commūnis, -e, *adj.,* in common, shared

compescō, -ere, compescuī, —, to confine, suppress, restrain, subdue

complexus, -ūs, *m.,* clasp, embrace; intercourse

concha, -ae, *f.,* shellfish, sea-shell

concipiō, -ere, -cēpī, -ceptum, to conceive (*a child, plan or idea*), produce, form

conclāve, -is, *n.,* enclosed space, room; public toilet

concurrō, -ere, -currī, -cursum, to run together, collide, strive, contend; coincide

condō, -ere, -didī, -ditum, to put in, store, hide, bury; found, establish; compose, write

coniunx, -iugis, *m./f.,* spouse, husband, wife

cōnsilium, -iī, *n.,* deliberation, advice, counsel; council; intention, purpose, judgment

cōnspicuus, -a, -um, *adj.,* clearly visible, remarkable, striking

cōnstō, -stāre, -stitī, —, to consist of; be fixed, established, manifest, agreed upon; cost

cōnsul, -ulis, *m.,* consul (*high-ranking magistrate*)

cōnsūmō, -ere, -sumpsī, -sumptum, to wear away, use up, exhaust, consume

convenit, -īre, convēnit, —, *impers.,* it is suitable, it is fitting; it is agreed

convictus, -ūs, *m.,* banquet, dinner-party

convīva, -ae, *m.,* fellow guest at a dinner-party

cor, cordis, *n.,* heart, mind, wits, intelligence

coram, *adv.,* face to face, in one's presence, openly, publicly

corda, -ae, *or* **chorda, -ae,**
f., string of a musical
instrument

Cornēlius, -ī *or* **-iī,** *m., proper*
name, Cornelius

cornū, -ūs, *n.,* horn (*of an*
animal, or as a substance);
tip, corner

corpus, -oris, *n.,* body

corvus, -ī, *m.,* raven

Cosmianus, -a, -um, *adj.,*
pertaining to Cosmus (*a*
well-known perfume-maker)

cras, *adv.,* tomorrow

crastinus, -a, -um, *adj.,*
pertaining to tomorrow,
tomorrow's

crēdō, -ere, crēdidī, crēditum,
to entrust, lend money to;
trust, believe, suppose

Cremōna, -ae, *f.,* Cremona (*city*
in northern Italy)

crescō, -ere, crēvī, crētum, to
arise, increase, grow

crīmen, -inis, *n.,* accusation,
indictment; matter for
reproach, misdeed, crime

crīsō (1), to shimmy the
hips (*suggesting sexual*
intercourse)

Crispus, -ī, *m., proper name,*
Crispus

crūs, crūris, *n.,* shin, leg

crux, crucis, *f.,* cross, crucifixion

cubō (1), to lie down, recline,
sleep

culex, -icis, *m.,* gnat, midge

cūlus, -ī, *m.,* anus, buttocks

cum, *prep. + abl.,* with

cum *or* **quom,** *conj.,* when,
since, although

cunctus, -a, -um, *adj.,* entire, all

cupīdō, -inis, *f.,* passionate
desire, longing, lust (*also*
personified as a god)

cupiō, -ere, cupīvī *or* **cupiī,**
cupītum, to desire, want,
wish for, long for

cūr, *interr.,* why? for what reason?

cūra, -ae, *f.,* anxiety, worry, care,
distress; solicitude, concern

Curius, -ī, *m., proper name,*
Curius

cutis, -is, *f.,* skin, hide

cycnus, -ī, *m.,* swan

cymbalum, -ī, *n.,* cymbal
(*usually in the pl.*)

Cynthia, -ae, *f., proper name,*
Cynthia

Damascēna, -ōrum, *n. pl.,*
plums (*pruna*) from
Damascus, damsons

damnum, -ī, *n.,* financial loss;
loss, deprivation, detriment

daps, dapis, *f.,* sacrificial meal;
feast, meal, banquet

dē, *prep. + abl.,* from, away from,
out of; about, concerning

dēbeō, -ēre, dēbuī, dēbitum, to
owe; ought, should

decet, -ēre, decuit, —, *impers.,*
it adorns; it is proper, right,
fitting

Deciānus, -ī, *m., pers. name,*
Decianus

dēcipiō, -ere, -cēpī, -ceptum,
to deceive, mislead, cheat

dēcoquō, -ere, -coxī, -coctum, to boil down, melt down; to squander, waste away

decus, -oris, *n.,* esteem, honor, distinction, glory

dēficiō, -ere, -fēcī, -fectum, to be lacking, run short, give out, come to an end

deinde *or* **dein,** *adv.,* afterwards, then, next

dēlectō (1), to delight, charm, amuse

dēlicia, -ae, *f. (usually pl.),* luxuries, delights; favorite, pet, plaything; caprices, whims

Dēlos, -ī, *f.,* Delos (*island in the Aegean*)

dēmēns, *gen.* **dēmentis,** *adj.,* out of one's mind, frenzied, insane

dēnique, *adv.,* finally, at last; in short, to sum up

dēns, dentis, *m.,* tooth, tusk

dentātus, -a, -um, *adj.,* having teeth, having prominent teeth

dēpōnō, -ere, -posuī, -positum, to put down, lay down, take off

dēprendo *or* **dēprehendō, -ere** *or* **-prehendere, -prendī** *or* **-prehendī, -prensum** *or* **-prehensum,** to seize, catch, discover

dēsīderium, -iī, *n.,* desire, longing

dēsum, dēesse, dēfuī, —, to be lacking, fail

dētrahō, -ere, -traxī, -tractum, to pull down, detach, withdraw

deus, -ī, *m.,* god, divinity

dextra, -ae, *f.,* the right hand

Diadūmenus, -ī, *m., proper name,* Diadumenus

Diaulus, -ī, *m., proper name,* Diaulus

dīcō, -ere, dīxī, dictum, to talk, speak, say, declare

diēs, diēī, *m./f.,* day, daylight

differō, -ferre, distulī, dīlātum, to scatter, disperse; postpone, defer

diffundō, -ere, -fūdī, -fūsum, to spread out, diffuse, expand

digitus, -ī, *m.,* finger, toe

dignus, -a, -um, *adj.,* suitable, worthy, deserving

dīligēns, *gen.* **dīligentis,** careful, attentive, scrupulous, diligent

dīmidius, -a, -um, *adj.,* half

Dindymus, -ī, *m., proper name,* Dindymus

dīrus, -a, -um, *adj.,* dreadful, frightful, dire

discō, -ere, didicī, —, to acquire knowledge or skill, get to know, learn

disiungō, -ere, -iunxī, -iunctum, *or* **diiungō, -iungere, -iunxī, -iunctum,** to separate, keep apart, distinguish

dissimulō (1), to conceal the identity of, disguise; pretend; ignore

distichum, -ī, *n.,* a poem of two lines, couplet

dītō (1), to enrich

diū, *adv.,* for a long time, long

dīves, *gen.* **dīvitis,** *adj.,* wealthy, rich

dīvitiae, -ārum, *f. pl.,* riches, abudance, wealth

dō, dare, dedī, datum, to give, grant, bestow

doceō, -ēre, docuī, doctum, to inform, demonstrate, teach, instruct

doctus, -a, -um, *adj.,* learned, scholarly, wise, expert

doleō, -ēre, doluī, dolitum, to suffer pain, be afflicted, grieve

dolor, -ōris, *m.,* pain, distress, anguish, grief

domina, -ae, *f.,* female head of the household, owner (*of a slave*), mistress

dominus, -ī, *m.,* male head of the household, owner (*of a slave*), master

domus, -ūs *or* **-ī,** *f.,* house, home

dōnō (1), to endow, reward with, grant, give to

dōnum, -ī, *n.,* gift, present, offering

dormītor, -ōris, *m.,* one who sleeps

dōs, dōtis, *f.,* dowry, endowment; talent, attribute

dubitō (1), to be in doubt, be uncertain, doubt, hesitate

dūcō, -ere, dūxī, ductum, to lead, conduct, take with one; marry; consider, think

dum, *conj.,* while, as long as; provided that; until

duo, -ae, -o, *adj.,* two

duplex, *gen.* **duplicis,** *adj.,* double, dual

dūrus, -a, -um, *adj.,* hard, firm, harsh; stubborn, pitiless

dux, ducis, *m.,* leader, guide, commander

ēbrius, -a, -um, *adj.,* drunk, intoxicated

ecce, *interj.,* see! look! behold!

ecferō *or* **efferō, ecferre** *or* **efferre, extulī, ēlātum,** to carry or bring out (*especially for burial*); send forth, emit

edō, esse, ēdī, ēsum, to eat, consume

ego, *gen.* **meī,** *pron.,* I

ēligō, -ere, ēlēgī, ēlectum, to pick out, select, choose

Ēlysius, -a, -um, *adj.,* pertaining to Elysium (*dwelling-place of the blessed dead*)

emō, -ere, ēmī, emptum, to buy, purchase

Endymiōn, -ōnis, *m., proper name,* Endymion

enim, *particle,* for; yes, because . . .; namely; that is to say

ēnsis, -is, *m.,* sword

epigramma, -matis *or* **-matos,** *n.,* inscription, epitaph; short poem, epigram

eques, equitis, *m.,* cavalryman, knight (*member of the equestrian order*)

equus, -ī, *m.,* horse

ergō *or* **ergo,** *particle,* for that reason, therefore, accordingly, then

ērigō, -ere, -rexī, -rectum, to raise, lift, elevate, erect, rouse

Erōs, Erōtis, *m., proper name,* Eros (*cf. 7.10.1*)

errō (1), to wander, roam, go astray, be mistaken

ērubescō, -ere, -rubuī, —, to blush, feel ashamed

esca, -ae, *f.,* food, bait

ēsuriō, -īre, —, -ītum, to be hungry

et, *conj. and adv.,* and, and what is more, and indeed; even, also

ex *or* **ē,** *prep. + abl.,* out of, from; as a result of

excidō, -ere, -cidī, —, to fall out, slip out; be lost, be forgotten

excipiō, -ere, -cēpī, -ceptum, to take out, set aside, exclude, except; to accept, receive, take

excutiō, -ere, -cussī, -cussum, to shake out, shake off, throw off

exhauriō, -īre, -hausī, -haustum, to drain, use up entirely, exhaust

exiguus, -a, -um, *adj.,* scanty, brief, meager

exolētus, -a, -um, *adj.,* grown up, adult; outdated, obsolete; (*as m. noun*) male prostitute

exōrō (1), to prevail upon, persuade, obtain by entreaty

explicō, -āre, -plicāvī *or* **-plicuī, -plicātum** *or* **-plicitum,** to unfold, untwine, extricate, make clear, explain

exprimō, -ere, -pressī, -pressum, to extract; reproduce, copy; express in words, describe

exspectō (1) *or* **expectō** (1), to wait for, expect, look forward to

extendō, -ere, -tendī, -tensum *or* **-tentum,** to stretch, distend, spread out, prolong, continue

extrā, *adv. or prep. + acc.,* outside, beyond the boundaries of, apart (from)

exuō, -ere, -uī, -ūtum, to take off, strip, deprive

Fabiānus, -ī, *m., proper name,* Fabianus

Fabricius, -ī, *m., proper name,* Fabricius

fābula, -ae, *f.,* talk, story, tale, legend; drama, play

Fabulla, -ae, *f., proper name,* Fabulla

Fabullus, -ī, *m., proper name,* Fabullus

facilis, -e, *adj.,* easy, tractable; indulgent, accommodating

facinus, -oris, *n.,* deed, misdeed, outrage, crime

faciō, -ere, fēcī, factum, to make, do; perform, bring about

factum, -ī, *n.,* deed, action, fact

fācundus, -a, -um, *adj.,* eloquent, fluent

Falernus, -a, -um, *adj.*,
Falernian (*pertaining to a
district in Campania*)

fallax, *gen.* **fallācis**, *adj.*,
deceitful, treacherous,
misleading, deceptive

fallō, -ere, fefellī, falsum,
to deceive, trick, mislead,
fool; disappoint; escape the
notice of

falsus, -a, -um, *adj.* erroneous,
untrue, false; deceitful,
treacherous, faithless

fāma, -ae, *f.*, news, rumor;
public opinion, talk;
reputation, glory, fame

Fannius, -ī, *m.*, *proper name*,
Fannius

fās, *indecl. n. noun*, that which
is right, fitting, proper
(*especially according to
religious tradition*)

fascia, -ae, *f.*, strip, ribbon, band

fastīdium, -ī, *n.*, distaste,
repulsion, disgust;
haughtiness, disdain, scorn

fateor, -ērī, fassus sum, to
acknowledge, avow, profess,
declare

fātum, -ī, *n.*, fate, destiny;
death, doom

fax, facis, *f.*, torch, firebrand

fēlīx, *gen.* **fēlīcis**, *adj.*, fruitful,
auspicious, blessed,
fortunate, successful,
prosperous, wealthy

fellō (1), to suck (*obscenity
denoting oral stimulation of
the penis*)

fēmina, -ae, *f.*, woman, female

femur, femoris *or* **feminis**, *n.*,
thigh, upper leg

fēnerātor, -ōris *or* **faenerātor,
-ōris**, *m.*, money-lender,
usurer

feritās, -tātis, *f.*, wildness,
fierceness, ferocity

ferō, ferre, tulī, lātum, to
carry, take, bring; undergo,
endure, sustain; relate, tell

ferrum, -ī, *n.*, iron; sword

ferus, -a, -um, *adj.*, wild,
untamed, savage, ferocious,
ruthless

fervēns, *gen.* **ferventis**, *adj.*,
intensely hot, boiling,
seething, ardent

Fīdentīnus, -ī, *m.*, *proper name*,
Fidentinus

fidēs, fideī, *f.*, trust, guarantee,
assurance, proof, good faith,
loyalty, credibility

fīdus, -a, -um, *adj.*, faithful,
loyal, devoted, trustworthy,
reliable

fīgō, -ere, fīxī, fīxum, to
drive in, transfix, pierce,
fasten

fīlia, -ae, *f.*, daughter

fīō, fīerī, factus sum, to occur,
happen, be made, become

Flaccus, -ī, *m.*, *proper name*,
Flaccus

flagellō (1), to whip, flog

flagrum, -ī, *n.*, whip, lash

Flāminius, -a, -um, *adj.*,
pertaining to the *gens
Flaminia*

fleō, -ēre, flēvī, flētum, to
weep, cry, lament

Flōrālia, -ium, *n. pl.*, the Floralia
(*festival held on April 28 in*
honor of the goddess Flora)

fluctus, -ūs, *m.*, wave, billow

fluō, -ere, fluxī, fluxum, to
flow, run, stream, overflow

focus, -ī, *m.*, hearth, fireplace

fodiō, -ere, fōdī, fossum, to
pierce, jab, dig

foedus, -a, -um, *adj.*, foul,
loathsome, repugnant,
frightful, severe, shameful,
vile

foedus, -eris, *n.*, formal
agreement, treaty, compact,
bond

fornix, -icis, *n.*, vault, arch;
brothel

fortasse, *adv.*, perhaps, possibly,
it may be

forte, *adv.*, by chance, as it
happens/happened

forum, -ī, *n.*, public square,
forum

frāter, frātris, *m.*, brother

frequēns, *gen.* frequentis,
adj., crowded, busy, densely
packed; assiduous, constant

frōns, frontis, *f.*, forehead,
brow; expression,
countenance; front

fruor, -ī, fructus sum, + *abl.*,
to enjoy (*the produce, use,*
or presence of); to derive
pleasure from

fuga, -ae, *f.*, the action of
running away, escape

fugiō, -ere, fūgī, —, to run
away, flee, escape, vanish; to
avoid, shun

fugitīvus, -a, -um, *adj.*, runaway, fugitive, escaping

fundō, -ere, fūdī, fūsum, to
pour; extend, spread out;
emit, distribute

furor, -ōris, *m.*, madness,
delirium, frenzy, passionate
desire

furtum, -ī, *n.*, robbery,
theft; secret action, stolen
pleasure; trick, deception

futuō, -ere, -uī, -ūtum, to
fuck (*primary obscenity for*
vaginal penetration)

futūtor, -ōris, *m.*, *primary*
obscenity for a man who
vaginally penetrates

Gādītānus, -a, -um, *adj.*, of or
pertaining to Gades (*modern*
Cadiz, Spain)

Gāius, -ī, *m.*, *proper name*, Gaius

Galatēa, -ēae, *f.*, *proper name*,
Galatea

Gallia, -ae, *f.*, Gaul

Gallicānus, -a, -um, *adj.*, of or
pertaining to Gaul

Gallus, -ī, *m.*, an inhabitant of
Gaul, a Gaul

gallus, -ī, *m.*, cock, rooster

gallus, -ī, *m.*, a castrated priest
of Cybele

Ganymēdēs, -is, *m.*, *proper*
name, Ganymede

Gargiliānus, -ī, *m.*, *proper*
name, Gargilianus

garum, -ī, *n.,* fish-sauce

gaudeō, -ēre, gavīsus sum, to be glad, be pleased, rejoice

gaudium, -ī, *n.,* joy, delight, gladness

Gellia, -ae, *f., proper name,* Gellia

Gemellus, -ī, *m., proper name,* Gemellus

gena, -ae, *f.,* cheek

gener, generī, *m.,* son-in-law

gēns, gentis, *f.,* nation, people; a Roman clan

Germānicus, -ī, *m., proper name,* Germanicus

gladius, -iī, *m.,* sword

Gorgō *or* **Gorgōn, Gorgōnis,** *f.,* a Gorgon (*especially Medusa*)

gracilis, -e, *adj.,* slender, slight, thin

grandis, -e, *adj.,* fully grown, mature; large, ample, great; loud

grātia, -ae, *f.,* goodwill; gratitude, thanks; popularity; agreeableness, charm

grātus, -a, -um, *adj.,* grateful, thankful; acceptable, pleasing, welcome, charming

gravis, -e, *adj.,* heavy, oppressive; relentless, harsh; serious, earnest; venerable, august

gula, -ae, *f.,* throat, gullet (*especially as the seat of the appetite or of taste*)

gulōsus, -a, -um, *adj.,* fond of food

gutta, -ae, *f.,* drop

habeō, -ēre, habuī, habitum, to have, possess, keep, hold; regard, look on as

habitō (1), to live in, inhabit, dwell in

haereō, -ēre, haesī, haesum, to adhere, stick, cling

hāmus, -ī, *m.,* hook, fish-hook

Harpȳia, -ae, *f.,* harpy (*mythic being*)

harundō, -inis, *f.,* reed; shepherd's pipe; pen

havē *or* **avē,** *interj.,* greetings! (*formal salutation*)

hēmitritaeos, -ī, *m.,* a semitertian fever (*with one paroxysm every day and a second, stronger one every two days*)

hērēs, hērēdis, *m./f.,* heir, successor

heri *or* **here,** *adv.,* yesterday

Hermaphrodītus, -ī, *m., proper name,* Hermaphroditus

heu, *interjection expressing sorrow, sadness or regret*

hic, haec, hoc, *adj. and pron.,* this

hilaris, -e *or* **hilarus, -a, -um,** *adj.,* cheerful, light-hearted, lively

hinc, *adv.,* from here, hence; on this side

Hippolytus, -ī, *m., proper name,* Hippolytus

historia, -ae, *f.,* investigation, research; written account of past events, history; story

hodiē, *adv.,* today

homō, -inis, *m.,* human being (*of either sex*), person

hōra, -ae, *f.,* hour

horribilis, -e, *adj.,* terrifying, dreadful; rough, uncouth

hospes, -itis, *m./f.,* guest, visitor; host, entertainer; stranger

hospitium, -ī, *n.,* the entertainment of guests, hospitality; guest accommodation

hostis, -is, *m./f.,* enemy

humus, -ī, *f.,* the surface of the earth, ground, soil

Hylās, -ae, *m., proper name,* Hylas

ī *imperative of* **eō**

iactō (1), to throw, hurl, toss about; speak boastingly of, brag about

iam, *adv.,* now, at this point, by now, by then

Ianthis, -idos, *f., proper name,* Ianthis

Īas, Īados, *f., proper name,* Ias

igitur, *adv.,* consequently, therefore, then, so

ignōrō (1), to be ignorant or unaware of

ignōscō, -ere, ignōvī, ignōtum, to forgive

ille, illa, illud, *adj. and pron.,* that

imāgō, -inis, *f.,* representation, likeness, image

imbrex, -icis, *m./f.,* semi-cylindrical tile (*placed over the joints between roof-tiles*); a filet of meat

immō, *particle,* rather, instead, on the contrary

immodicus, -a, -um, *or* **inmodicus, -a, -um,** *adj.,* not exercising restraint, immoderate, excessive, extravagant

imperō (1), to order, command, exercise authority over, rule over

īmus, -a, -um, *adj.,* lowest, deepest, innermost, bottommost

in, *prep. + acc.,* into, to, towards, against, for; *prep. + abl.,* in, on, amidst, among

inchoō *or* **incohō** (1), to start forming, begin, initiate

incomptus, -a, -um, *adj.,* disshevelled, untidy

incustōdītus, -a, -um, *adj.,* not watched over, unsupervised, unguarded

inde, *adv.,* from there, thence, from that time; therefore, then

indecēns, *gen.* **indecentis,** *adj.,* unfitting, unsightly, unattractive

Indicus, -a, -um, *adj.,* Indian, of India

indulgeō, -ēre, indulsī, indultum, to be indulgent or lenient, show kindness, indulge in

infandus, -a, -um, *adj.,* unspeakable, monstrous, shocking

inferior, -ior, -ius, *compar. adj.,* lower, below, inferior, worse

infernus, -a, -um, *adj.,* below, lower; pertaining to the underworld

ingenium, -iī, *n.,* temperament, disposition, intellect, talent

ingēns, *gen.* **ingentis,** *adj.,* huge, vast, powerful

ingenuus, -a, -um, *adj.,* free-born, befitting a free-born person; honorable, generous

ingrātus, -a, -um, *adj.,* ungrateful, unappreciative; displeasing, unpopular, disagreeable

inguen, -inis, *n.,* groin, sexual organs

inlaesus, -a, -um *or* **illaesus, -a, -um,** *adj.,* unharmed, uninjured, intact

inquam, *defective verb,* to say

insānia, -ae, *f.,* delusion, folly, frenzy

inscrībō, -ere, -scrīpsī, -scriptum, to write on, inscribe, entitle, name

insequor, -ī, -secūtus sum, to pursue, chase, follow

insidiae, -ārum, *f. pl.,* ambush, treacherous attack, plot

inspiciō, -ere, -spexī, -spectum, to examine visually, look at, investigate

instō, -stāre, -stitī, —, to loom, threaten, be urgent, be pressing

insum, -esse, -fuī, —, to be in or on, be among, be present in

inveniō, -īre, -vēnī, -ventum, to encounter, come upon, find, discover; devise, plan

invideō, -ēre, -vīdī, -vīsum, to regard with ill will, be jealous of, begrudge

invidiōsus, -a, -um, *adj.,* arousing hatred or envy, odious, unpopular

invītō (1), to provide with hospitality, invite to entertainment, request

iocōsus, -a, -um, *adj.,* fond of jokes, jesting, fun

iocus, -ī, *m.,* joke, jest

Iōnes, -um, *m. pl.,* Ionians, inhabitants of Ionia (*coastal region of Asia Minor*)

Iovis. *See* **Iuppiter**

ipse, ipsa, ipsum, *adj. or pron.,* himself/herself/itself (*as opposed to others*), in person, the very one

is, ea, id, *adj. or pron.,* this, that

Issa, -ae, *f., proper name,* Issa

īsse. *See* **eō**

iste, ista, istud, *adj. or pron.,* this, that

Ītalia, -ae, *f.,* Italy

iubeō, -ēre, iussī, iussum, to order, tell, ask to, direct, decree

iūcundus, -a, -um, *adj.,* pleasant, agreeable, delightful, congenial

iūgerum, -ī *or* **-is,** *n.,* a measure of land; (*pl.*) expanse of land

iugulum, -ī, *n.,* throat

Iūlius, -iī, *m., proper name,* Julius

iungō, -ere, iunxī, iunctum, to join, connect, unite

Iuppiter, Iovis, *m., proper name,* Jupiter (*king of the gods*)

iūs, iūris, *n.,* law, legal system; one's due, one's right, prerogative

iuvenālis, -e, *adj.,* pertaining to a young person, youthful, in one's prime

iuvenis, -is, *m.,* young person (*of either sex*), young man

iuvō, -āre, iūvī, iūtum, to help, assist, benefit, be of use to; give pleasure to, gratify

Labiēnus, -ī, *m., proper name,* Labienus

lābor, -ī, lapsus sum, to glide, slip, slide, flow

labor, -ōris, *m.,* work, labor, toil, hardship

labrum, -ī, *n.,* lip

lacerus, -a, -um, *adj.,* mutilated, mangled, lacerated

Lacō *or* **Lacōn, -ōnis,** *m.,* a Laconian, Spartan

lacrima, -ae, *f.,* tear, (*pl.*) weeping

lactūca, -ae, *f.,* lettuce

Laetīnus, -ī, *m., proper name,* Laetinus

laetitia, -ae, *f.,* joy, gladness, pleasure

lagōna, -ae, *f.,* flask, flagon, wine-flask

lapillus, -ī, *m.,* small stone, pebble, gem

lapsus, -a, -um. *See* **lābor**

largior, -īrī, -ītus sum, to give generously, lavish, bestow

lascīvus, -a, -um, *adj.,* playful, frisky, mischievous, naughty

lateō, -ēre, -uī, —, to hide, be invisible, go unobserved

Latius, -a, -um, *adj.,* Latin, pertaining to Latium (*region of Italy where Rome is located*)

latus, -eris, *n.,* side, flank; area, region, quarter

laudō (1), to praise, commend, speak well of

laurea, -ae, *f.,* laurel tree, branch or wreath of laurel (*symbol of victory*)

Laureolus, -ī, *m., proper name,* Laureolus

laus, laudis, *f.,* praise, commendation; renown

laxus, -a, -um, *adj.,* spacious, ample, loose, relaxed

lector, -ōris, *m.,* one who reads, reader

lectulus, -ī, *m.,* couch, bed

Lēdaeus, -a, -um, *adj.,* pertaining to Leda

legō, -ere, lēgī, lectum, to gather, collect, choose, select; to read, peruse

leō, -ōnis, *m.,* lion

lepus, -oris, *m.,* hare

Lesbia, -ae, *f., proper name,* Lesbia

levō (1), to lift up, pick up; to relieve, refresh

levis, -e, *adj.,* light, mild, slight, insignificant, trivial

lēvis, -e, *adj.,* smooth, soft, polished

lex, lēgis, *f.,* law, statute; rule, regulation; principle, condition, terms

libellus, -ī, *m.,* small volume, book; document, dispatch, report

liber, librī, *m.,* book, volume, scroll, document

lībertus, -ī, *m.,* freed slave, freedman

libō (1), to pour a libation; sip, touch lightly, graze, skim

lībra, -ae, *f.,* pound; pair of scales, balance

licet, -ēre, licuit *or* **licitum est,** *impers.,* it is permitted, one may; although (+ *subjunctive*)

līmen, -inis, *n.,* threshold, doorway, entrance

lingua, -ae, *f.,* tongue, language

Linus, -ī, *m., proper name,* Linus (*cf. 7.10.1*)

līs, lītis, *f.,* dispute at law, lawsuit; dispute, quarrel

litūra, -ae, *f.,* blot, smear, smudge; erasure or correction (*on a wax tablet*)

lītus, -oris, *n.,* shore, coast

Līvius, -ī *or* **-iī,** *m., proper name,* Livius, Livy

locuplēs, *gen.* **locupētis,** *adj.,* wealthy, rich

longē, *adv.,* a long way, far, far off; by a large margin, greatly

longinquus, -a, -um, *adj.,* far away, remote

longus, -a, -um, *adj.,* long, lengthy, long-lasting

loquax, *gen.* **loquācis,** *adj.,* talkative, loquacious, verbose, articulate

loquor, -ī, locūtus sum, to talk, speak, converse

Lucānus, -ī, *m., proper name,* Lucan

Lucēnsis, -is, *m., proper name,* Lucensis

Lucrīnus, -a, -um, *adj.,* pertaining to the Lucrine Lake (*a lagoon near Baiae*)

lucrum, -ī, *n.,* gain, profit

ludibrium, -iī, *n.,* plaything, toy; object of derision, laughing-stock; mockery, derision

lūdō, -ere, lūsī, lūsum, to play, amuse oneself, have fun; tease, trick

lūgeō, -ēre, luxī, luctum, to mourn, grive, lament, bewail

lūgubris, -e, *adj.,* sad, grievous, gloomy

lupa, -ae, *f.,* she-wolf; female prostitute

lupus, -ī, *m.,* wolf; a type of fish (*similar to the bass*)

Lupus, -ī, *m., proper name,* Lupus

lūsus, -ūs, *m.,* game, playfulness, amusement, joke

lux, lūcis, *f.,* light, daylight; darling (*term of endearment*)

luxuria, -ae, *or* **luxuriēs, -iēī,** *f.,* luxury, indulgence, extravagance

luxuriōsus, -a, -um, *adj.,*
luxuriant, self-indulgent,
extravagant

Lycōris, -idis *or* **-idos,** *f., proper*
name, Lycoris

macrescō, -ere, —, —, to
become thin, waste away

macte, *vocative of adj. with*
estō *expressed or implied,* be
honored with, be blessed for,
hurrah for (+ *abl.*)

madeō, -ēre, —, —, to be wet or
moist; to be drunk

Maecēnās, -ātis, *m., proper*
name, Maecenas

maeror, -ōris, *n.,* grief, sorrow,
mourning

maestus, -a, -um, *adj.,* sad,
mournful, gloomy

magis, *adv.,* to a greater extent,
more; rather, instead

magister, -trī, *m.,* chief officer,
manager; teacher, professor

magnus, -a, -um, *adj.,* great,
big, large, powerful, eminent

Magulla, -ae, *f., proper name,*
Magulla

maior, -ior, -us, *compar. of*
magnus

malignus, -a, -um, *adj.,*
ungenerous, grudging,
spiteful, unkind

mālō, mālle, mālui, —, to
prefer

malus, -a, -um, *adj.,* painful,
wicked, hostile, unfavorable,
bad

mamma, -ae, *f.,* breast, udder

Mamurra, -ae, *m., proper*
name, Mamurra

māne, *adv.,* in the morning

Mantua, -ae, *f.,* Mantua (*city*
in northern Italy, considered
Vergil's birthplace)

manus, -ūs, *f.,* hand; troop, band

mappa, -ae, *f.,* cloth, towel,
napkin

mare, -is, *n.,* sea, sea-water

marītus, -ī, *m.,* husband, mate

marmor, -oris, *n.,* marble

marmoreus, -a, -um, *adj.,* made
of marble, resembling marble
(*especially in whiteness*)

Marō, -ōnis, *m., proper name,*
Maro

Marōnilla, -ae, *f., proper name,*
Maronilla

Marsus, -ī, *m., proper name,*
Marsus

Martiālis, -is, *m., proper name,*
Martialis, Martial

Martius, -a, -um, *adj.,*
pertaining to Mars

masturbātor, -ōris, *m.,* one
who masturbates

māter, -tris, *f.,* mother; matron

Mathō, -ōnis, *m., proper name,*
Matho

matrōna, -ae, *f.,* a married
woman, matron, wife

mātūtīnus, -a, -um, *adj.,*
pertaining to the early
morning

Mausōlēum, -ēī, *n.,* the
Mausoleum (*tomb of*
Mausolus at Halicarnassus);
any large and ornate tomb

māvīs. *See* **mālō**

maximus, -a, -um, *superl. of* **magnus**

Maximus, -ī, *m., proper name,* Maximus

medicus, -ī, *m.,* doctor, physician

mediocris, -e, *adj.,* moderate in size or quality, middling, commonplace, ordinary, average

medius, -a, -um, *adj.,* central, middle, intervening

mel, mellis, *n.,* honey

melior, -ius, *compar. of* **bonus**

membrāna, -ae, *f.,* membrane, skin; parchment

membrum, -ī, *n.,* body part, limb; division, section

mementō, *imperative of* **meminī, meminisse,** to remember, keep in mind, recall

memorandus, -a, -um, *adj.,* worthy of being spoken of, noteworthy, memorable

Memphis, -is, *f.,* Memphis (*ancient city of Egypt*)

mēns, mentis, *f.,* mind, intention, attitude, inclination

mēnsa, -ae, *f.,* table, table-top; dish, course, meal

mentior, -īrī, mentītus sum, to tell a falsehood, lie; feign, simulate, pretend to be

mentula, -ae, *f.,* dick, cock (*primary obscenity for the penis*)

meretrīx, -trīcis, *f.,* female prostitute

merum, -ī, *n.,* pure wine (*not mixed with water*), neat wine

messis, -is, *f.,* reaping of crops, harvest

metuō, -ere, -uī, -ūtum, to fear, be afraid of, view with alarm

meus, -a, -um (*vocative* **mī**), *adj.,* my, my dear

mille, *pl.* **mīlia,** *indecl. noun and adj.,* thousand

minister, -trī, *m.,* servant, assistant; attendant, subordinate

minus, *adv.,* less, to a smaller extent, not fully

mīrāculum, -ī, *n.,* an amazing object or sight, marvel, wonder

mīror, -ārī, -ātus sum, to be surprised or amazed, marvel at, admire

misceō, -ēre, -uī, mixtum, to mix, blend, combine; mix up, muddle

miser, -era, -erum, *adj.,* unfortunate, pitiable, wretched, poor; grievous, distressing

mittō, -ere, mīsī, missum, to release, set free, discharge, let fly; send, dispatch

modo, *adv.,* just, only, just now, only recently

moecha, -ae, *f.,* married woman with a lover, adulteress

moechus, -ī, *m.,* lover of a married woman, adulterer

mōlēs, -is, *f.,* large mass, massive structure, burden, exertion

mollis, -e, *adj.,* soft, tender, voluptuous, effeminate

moneō, -ēre, -uī, -itum, to remind, advise, recommend, warn

Monobiblos, -ī, *m.,* book in a single volume (*title of a book of Propertius' poetry*)

mōns, montis, *m.,* mountain, hill

mōnstrum, -ī, *n.,* portent, prodigy, monstrosity, atrocity, monster

monumentum, -ī, *n.,* tomb, memorial; document, record

mōriō, -ōnis, *m.,* idiot, fool (*hired or kept as an entertainer*)

morior, -ī, mortuus sum, to die, perish

mōrum, -ī, *n.,* black mulberry

mōs, mōris, *m.,* custom, usage, tradition, manner of doing something; (*usually pl.*) habits, disposition, character

moveō, -ēre, mōvī, mōtum, to move, agitate, disturb

mullus, -ī, *m.,* red mullet (*type of fish*)

mulsum, -ī, *m.,* mead

multus, -a, -um, *adj.* numerous, many, much

mūnificus, -a, -um, *adj.,* generous, bountiful, munificent

mūnus, -eris, *n.,* task, duty; present, gift

muraena, -ae, *or* **murēna, -ae,** *f.,* moray eel

murrina, -ōrum, *n. pl.,* vases (*made of fluorspar or agate*)

Mūsa, -ae, *f.,* Muse

mūtuus, -a, -um, *adj.,* on loan; mutual, reciprocal

Naevia, -ae, *f., proper name,* Naevia

nam, *particle,* certainly, to be sure; for, because; moreover

narrō (1), to tell, say, describe, tell about

nascor, -ī, nātus sum, to be born, come into being

nāsus, -ī, *m., or* **nāsum, -ī,** *n.,* nose; sharp wit

nātus, -ī, *m.,* male offspring, son

nē, *conj. introducing negative purpose clauses, negative wishes, etc.,* not, lest

nec *or* **neque,** *conj.,* and not, and yet not, but not; **neque . . . neque:** neither . . . nor

necesse, *adv. used predicatively with* **est,** essential, inevitable, necessary

nectareus, -a, -um, *adj.,* pertaining to nectar (*the drink of the gods*), sweet as nectar

nefās, *indecl. noun,* impious act, offence against divine law, wicked deed

negō (1), to deny, refuse, withold, say no, say that . . . not

nēmō, nēminis, *pron.,* nobody, no one

nēquam, *indecl. adj.,* worthless, mischievous, naughty

neque. *See* **nec**

nēquior, -ius, *compar. of*
nēquam

nēquitia, -ae, *f.,*
naughtiness, wantonness,
mischievousness

Nerō, -ōnis, *m., proper name,*
Nero

nesciō, -īre, -īvī *or* **-iī, -ītum,**
not to know, to be unfamiliar
with or unaware of

Nestor, -oris, *m., proper name,*
Nestor

nēve *or* **neu,** *conj. adding a*
negative clause, nor, and that
. . . not

niger, -gra, -grum, *adj.,* dark,
shadowy, black

nihil *or* **nīl,** *indecl. pron.,*
nothing; (*used adverbially*)
in no way, not at all

Nīlus, -ī, *m.,* the Nile River

nimis, *adv.,* too much,
excessively, very much

nimius, -a, -um, *adj.,* too great,
excessive, superabundant

nisi, *conj.,* except if, unless, if
not, other than, except

nītor, -ī, nīxus sum *or* **nīsus**
sum, to lean on, rely on;
strain, struggle, strive

nōbilis, -e, *adj.,* well known,
famous; illustrious, noble,
well-born

nocēns, *gen.* **nocentis,** *adj.,*
injurious; guilty (*of a crime*
or misdeed)

noceō, -ēre, -uī, -itum, to injur,
hurt, damage

nōlō, nōlle, noluī, —, to be
unwilling, not to want

nōmen, -inis, *n.,* name, word,
designation; noun

nōn, *adv.,* not

nōndum, *adv.,* not yet

nōs, *gen.* **nostrum** *or* **nostrī,**
pron., we, us

noscō, -ere, nōvī, nōtum, to get to
know, find out; (*in pf. tenses*) to
be familiar with, know

noster, -tra, -trum, *adj.,* our

notō (1), to put a sign on, make
a mark on, mark, single out,
stigmatize

nōtus, -a, -um, *adj.,* known,
familiar, widely known

novem, *indecl. adj.,* nine

nox, noctis, *f.,* night, night-
time, darkness, gloom

nūbilus, -a, -um, *adj.,* cloudy,
overcast, clouded, gloomy

nūbō, -ere, nupsī, nuptum, to
marry (*describing the bride's*
role)

nūdus, -a, -um, *adj.,* nude,
unclothed, exposed, bare

nūgae, -ārum, *f. pl.,* worthless
things, frivolities, trifles

nullus, -a, -um, *adj.,* not any,
no, none

Numa, -ae, *m., proper name,*
Numa (*second king of Rome*)

numerō (1), to add up, count,
reckon, enumerate

numerus, -ī, *m.,* sum, total,
number

nummus, -ī, *m.,* coin, sesterce;
(*especially pl.*) money, cash

numquam, *adv.,* at no time, never

numquid, *interr. particle,* surely not?, can it really be? (*anticipating a negative answer*)

nunc, *adv.,* now, at this/that time, (but) as it is

nūper, *adv.,* recently, not long ago

nuptiae, -ārum, *f. pl.,* marriage, wedding

nusquam, *adv.,* nowhere, under no circumstances

ō, *interj., with vocative,* O; *expressing admiration, pleasure, horror, desire, etc.,* O that, O what (a)

obscūrus, -a, -um, *adj.,* dim, dark, obscure; little known, undistinguished

Ōceanus, -ī, *m.,* the ocean (*especially the Atlantic*)

oculus, -ī, *m.,* eye

ōdī, ōdisse, ōsum, to dislike, have an aversion to, hate

Oedipodēs, -ae, *acc.* -**ēn,** *or* **Oedipūs, -odis** *or* -**odos,** *or* **Oedipus, -ī,** *m.,* Oedipus (*mythic character*)

offendō, -ere, offendī, offensum, to strike against, come upon; upset, displease, offend

ōlim, *adv.,* once, in olden times (*in the past*); one day (*in the fut.*)

Ōlus, -ī, *m., pers. name,* Olus (*alternative form of* **Aulus, -ī**)

omnis, -e, *adj.,* all, entire, every

onus, -eris, *n.,* burden, load

ops, opis, *f.,* power, ability; (*pl.*) resources, wealth

optō (1), to desire, pray for; choose

opus, -eris, *n.,* work, effort; creation; building, structure

orbus, -a, -um, *adj.,* deprived of, bereft of (*especially by death*); orphaned; childless

ordō, -inis, *m.,* row, line, series, pattern, order

orior, -īrī, ortus sum, to rise, begin, come into existence, be born of

os, ossis, *n.,* bone

ōs, ōris, *n.,* mouth, opening; face, gaze

ōsculum, -ī, *n.,* mouth, lips; kiss

ostreum, -ī, *n., or* **ostrea, -ae,** *f.,* oyster

ōtiōsus, -a, -um, *adj.,* having ample leisure, inactive; undisturbed, tranquil

ōtium, -ī, *n.,* freedom from business or work, leisure, inactivity, idleness; tranquillity

ovis, -is, *m./f.,* sheep

paciscor, -ī, pactus sum, to negotiate, agree to, bargain, settle

paene, *adv.,* almost, all but, practically

Paetus, -ī, *m., proper name,* Paetus

pāgina, -ae, *f.,* column or page of writing

Palladius, -a, -um, *adj.,* pertaining to Pallas Athena (Minerva)

pallium, -ī, *n.,* cloak; blanket, bedsheet

palumbus, -ī, *m., or* **palumbēs, -is,** *m./f.,* wood-pigeon

papilla, -ae, *f.,* nipple, teat

pār, *gen.* **paris,** matching, similar, equal in worth, comparable

parcō, -ere, pepercī, —, to refrain from, spare, act mercifully (+ *dat.*)

parēns, -ntis, *m./f.,* parent, father, mother

pariō, -ere, peperī, partum, to give birth to, give rise to, produce

Paris, -idis, *m., proper name,* Paris

parō (1), to supply, provide; obtain, acquire, get; make ready, prepare

Parthenopaeus, -ī, *m., proper name,* Parthenopaeus

Parthus, -a, -um, *adj.,* Parthian, pertaining to Parthia (*approximately modern Iran*) or its inhabitants

partus, -a, -um. *See* **pariō**

parum, *adv.,* too little, not enough, insufficiently

parvus, -a, -um, *adj.,* small, little; insignificant, unimportant

passer, -eris, *m.,* sparrow

passus, -ūs, *m.,* pace, step, stride

pateō, -ēre, patuī, —, to be open, be exposed, be visible; extend, stretch, spread out

pater, -tris, *m.,* father

paternus, -a, -um, *adj.,* of one's father, pertaining to a father, paternal

patior, -ī, passus sum, to experience, undergo, be subjected to, put up with, allow

paucī, -ae, -a, *adj.,* few

Paula, -ae, *f., proper name,* Paula

Paulus, -ī, *m., proper name,* Paulus

pauper, *gen.* **pauperis,** *adj.,* not wealthy, poor

paupertās, -tātis, *f.,* poverty

paveō, -ēre, —, —, to be frightened, be terrified

pax, pācis, *f.,* pact, settlement, peace

peccō (1), to blunder, make a mistake, act incorrectly, do wrong

pectorālis, -e, *adj.,* of or for the breast

pectus, -oris, *n.,* chest, breast; soul, mind

pecūnia, -ae, *f.,* wealth, money

pēdīcō *or* **paedīcō** (1), to fuck in the ass (*primary obscenity for anal penetration*)

pēdīcō, -ōnis, *or* **paedīcō, -ōnis,** *m., primary obscenity for a man who anally penetrates others*

pēgma, -atis, *n.,* platform, scaffold

pellis, -is, *f.,* skin, hide

pendeō, -ēre, pependī, —, to be suspended, be perched, hang

per, *prep.* + *acc.,* through, across, throughout, by means of; by (*in oaths*)

perditus, -a, -um, *adj.,* ruined, lost, desperate, depraved

perdō, -ere, -didī, -ditum, to ruin, destroy; lose, waste, dissipate

peregrīnus, -a, -um, *adj.,* foreign, alien

perennis, -e, *adj.,* continuing throughout the year, constant, uninterrupted, enduring

perhibeō, -ēre, -hibuī, -hibitum, to present, bestow, give; regard, repute

perimō, -ere, -ēmī, -emptum, to destroy, annihilate

permittō, -ere, -mīsī, -missum, to grant, permit, allow

persōna, -ae, *f.,* mask (*especially one worn by actors*), character, role, person

pertinet, -ēre, -uit, —, *impers.,* to pertain to, have to do with, be the concern of

pēs, pedis, *m.,* foot

petō, -ere, petīvī *or* **petiī, petītum,** to head for, aim at, strive for; request, ask for

pexus, -a, -um, *adj.,* neatly combed, well brushed

Philētus, -ī, *m., proper name,* Philetus

Phoebus, -ī, *m., proper name,* Phoebus

pictus, -a, -um, *adj.,* painted, colored

Pīeris, -idos, *f.,* daughter of Pierus (*i.e., a Muse*)

pietās, -tātis, *f.,* dutiful respect, devotion

piger, -gra, -grum, *adj.,* sluggish, torpid, lazy, idle

piget, -ēre, piguit *or* **pigitum est,** *impers.,* to affect with revulsion or displeasure

pigritia, -ae, *f.,* sluggishness, indolence, laziness

pilō (1), to pluck, depilate

pīlum, -ī, *n.,* throwing-spear, javelin (*used by the Roman legionary*); (**centūriō**) **prīmī pīlī,** the senior centurion of a legion, the *primipilus*

pilus, -ī, *m.,* hair (*on the body*)

pinguis, -e, *adj.,* fat, plump; fatty, greasy; luxuriant, rich

pinna, -ae, *f.,* feather, wing

piscis, -is, *m.,* fish

pius, -a, -um, *adj.,* dutiful, conscientious, upright, devoted, loyal

placeō, -ēre, -uī, -itum, to be pleasing or acceptable, find favor

plēnus, -a, -um, *adj.,* full, abundant, satisfied

plōrō (1), to wail, cry out, lament, weep

plūrēs, -ā, *adj.,* more, further, more; several, a number of

plūs, plūris, *n.,* a great amount or number, more

poena, -ae, *f.,* penalty, punishment

poēta, -ae, *m.,* poet

pōnō, -ere, posuī, positum, to place, set, put; set aside, put down, lay down

Ponticus, -ī, *m., proper name,* Ponticus

populus, -ī, *m.,* a people, the people, the public

porcus, -ī, *m.,* male pig

porrigō, -ere, porrexī, porrectum, to stretch out, extend, prolong; to hold out, offer, present

porticus, -ūs, *f.,* portico, colonnade, covered walk

portō (1), to transport, convey, carry, bear, bring

poscō, -ere, poposcī, —, to demand, call for, summon, require

possum, posse, potuī, —, to be able, be capable of, be possible, can

post, *prep. + acc.,* behind, after

Postumus, -ī, *m., proper name,* Postumus

pote *or* **potis,** *indecl. adj.,* capable of being, able to be

potēns, *gen.* **potentis,** *adj.,* potent, efficacious; powerful, influential

praebeō, -ēre, -uī, -itum, to present, offer, provide, supply

praeda, -ae, *f.,* booty, plunder, loot; prey, game

praelegō, -ere, -lēgī, -lectum, to read aloud, recite

praemium, -iī, *n.,* payment, reward, prize

praeses, praesidis, *m.,* guardian, custodian

praestō, -stāre, -stitī *or* **-stāvī, -stitum** *or* **-stātum,** to be outstanding, excel; supply, provide

praetereō, -īre, -iī *or* **-īvī, -itum,** to pass by, go past, omit, neglect

precor (1), to ask or pray for, beg, implore

pressus, -a, -um, *adj.,* firm, hard; compressed, dense; in quick succession

Priamus, -ī, *m., proper name,* Priam

Priāpus, -ī, *m., proper name,* Priapus

prīmus, -a, -um, *adj.,* first, earliest, foremost, leading, chief, principal

princeps, principis, *n.,* leading figure, chief man (*often referring to the Roman emperor*)

prior, -us, *compar. adj.,* in front, ahead; previous, prior, the one before

Priscus, -ī, *m., proper name,* Priscus

prō, *prep. + abl.,* in front of, on behalf of, in the interests of, in place of, in the capacity of

prōderit. *See* **prōsum**

Promētheus, -eī *or* **-eos,** *m.,*
   proper name, Prometheus
Propertius, -ī *or* **-iī,** *m., proper*
   name, Propertius
propior, -ior, -ius, *compar. adj.,*
   nearer, closer
propter, *prep. + acc.,* near, close
   to; because of, on account of
proptereā, *adv.,* on account of
   that, consequently, therefore
Prōserpina, -ae, *f., proper*
   name, Proserpina
prōsiliō, -īre, -uī, —, to rush
   forward, spring forth, gush
prōsum, prōdesse, prōfuī, —,
   to be of use, be helpful, be
   beneficial (+ *dat.*)
prōtinus, *adv.,* straight away, at
   once, immediately
Prūdēns, -ntis, *m., proper*
   name, Prudens
prūnum, -ī, *n.,* plum
prūriō, -īre, —, —, to itch, be
   sexually excited
psittacus, -ī, *m.,* parrot
Publius, -ī *or* **-iī,** *m., proper*
   name, Publius
pudet, -ēre, puduit *or* **puditum**
   est, *impers.,* to fill with
   shame, make ashamed
pudīcus, -a, -um, *adj.,* sexually
   pure, chaste
pudor, -ōris, *m.,* feeling of
   shame, sense of propriety,
   decency, scrupulousness
puella, -ae, *f.,* girl, maiden, young
   woman; daughter; female slave
puer, -ī, *m.,* boy, lad, young
   man; son; male slave

pulcher, -chra, -chrum, *adj.,*
   beautiful, lovely; fine,
   choice, splendid, noble
pullus, -ī, *m.,* young horse, foal;
   young chicken, chick
pulsō (1), to strike repeatedly,
   beat, knock on, bang on
pūmex, -icis, *m.,* volcanic rock,
   pumice
pūrus, -a, -um, *adj.,* clean,
   pure, unadorned; blameless,
   innocent
putō (1), to tidy, prune; estimate,
   consider, think, suppose
pȳramis, -idis *or* **-idos,** *f.,*
   pyramid

qua. *See* **quis, qua, quid**
quā, *f. abl. sing. of* **quī, quae,**
   quod
quadrāns, -ntis, *m., coin having*
   the value of one-fourth of
   an **as**
quaerō, -ere, quaesīvī,
   quaesītum, to seek, look for;
   inquire about, ask
quālis, -e, *adj.,* of what kind?
   what kind of? the kind that,
   such as (*correlated with*
   tālis)
quāliter, *adv.,* the way in which,
   just as
quam, *f. acc. sing. of* **quī, quae,**
   quod *or* **quis, qua, quid**
quandō, *adv.,* when?, when; in
   view of the fact that, since
quantuluscumque, -acumque,
   -umcumque, *adj.,* however
   small, however little

quantus, -a, -um, *interr. and adj.,* how big? as big as (*correlated with* **tantus**)

quārē, *adv.,* why?, whereby, wherefore, hence

quattuor, *indecl.,* four

querēla, -ae, *or* **querella, -ae,** *f.,* complaint, protest

queror, -ī, questus sum, to complain, protest

querulus, -a, -um, *adj.,* full of complaints, fretful, querulous

quī, quae, quod, *rel. pron.,* which, that, who

quīdam, quaedam, quoddam, *adj.,* a particular, a certain

quiētus, -a, -um, *adj.,* at rest, quiet, peaceable

quindeciēs *or* **-iēns,** *adv.,* fifteen times

quippe, *particle,* for, as is to be expected; namely; indeed

quis, qua, quid, *unaccented form of* **aliquis, aliqua, aliquid** (*used after* **sī, nisi, num, nē**), any, some, anyone, anything

quis, quid, *interrog. pron.,* who? what?

quisquam, quicquam *or* **quidquam,** *pron.,* any, anyone (at all)

quisquis, quicquid *or* **quidquid,** whoever, whatever

quō, *m. or n. abl. sing. of* **quī, quae, quod**

quod, *n. nom. or acc. sing. of* **quī, quae, quod**

quod, *conj.,* as to which; that, the fact that

quoque, *adv.,* likewise, besides, also, as well

quot, *interr. or rel.,* how many? as many as

radiō (1), to shine, gleam, radiate

radius, -iī, *m.,* a ray of light, spoke

rapidus, -a, -um, *adj.,* rapid, quick, swiftly moving

rapiō, -ere, rapuī, raptum, to seize, carry off, snatch up

rārus, -a, -um, *adj.,* sparse, infrequent, scarce; rare, uncommon

rātiō, -ōnis, *f.,* calculation, reckoning; explanation, reason; system, method

recitō (1), to read out loud, recite (*especially before an audience*)

recumbō, -ere, -cubuī, —, to lie down, recline (*to sleep or to dine*)

reddō, -ere, reddidī, redditum, to give back, restore, return, pay back, hand over

redeō, -īre, rediī, reditum, to come back, go back, return

referō, referre, rettulī, relātum, to bring back, report, recall, mention

religō (1), to tie, bind fast, make fast, secure

relinquō, -ere, -līquī, -lictum, to leave, abandon, leave behind

remaneō, -ēre, -mānsī, —, to remain, stay behind, be left

remittō, -ere, -mīsī, -missum, to send back, give back; release, let go

repellō, -ere, reppulī, repulsum, to push away, drive back, repel, reject

repente, *adv.,* without warning, suddenly, all at once

reperiō, -īre, repperī, repertum, to find, discover, devise

replētus, -a, -um, *adj.,* full (+*gen. or abl.*)

repōnō, -ere, -posuī, -positum, to put back, replace, restore

requiescō, -ere, -quiēvī, -quiētum, to take repose, rest

requīrō, -ere, -quīsīvī, -quīsītum, to look for, seek; ask or inquire about

rēs, reī, *f.,* property, wealth; object, thing; fact, deed, matter

respiciō, -ere, -spexī, -spectum, to look back; heed, have regard for, show concern for

revocō (1), to summon back, recall; return the hospitality of

rex, rēgis, *m.,* ruler, king; great man (*respectful title*)

rhīnocerōs, -ōtis, *m.,* rhinoceros

rhoncus, -ī, *m.,* snort

rideō, -ēre, rīsī, rīsum, to laugh, laugh at, make fun of

rīma, -ae, *f.,* crack, fissure

rixa, -ae, *f.,* brawl, altercation, struggle

rogō (1), to ask, request, invite

Rōma, -ae, *f.,* Rome

Rōmānus, -a, -um, *adj.,* Roman

roseus, -a, -um, *adj.,* made of roses, rose-colored

ruber, -bra, -brum, *adj.,* red, orange

rudis, -e, *adj.,* unfinished, unsophisticated, untrained, inexperienced

Rūfus, -ī, *m., proper name,* Rufus

rūgōsus, -a, -um, *adj.,* full of wrinkles, folds, or creases

rūpēs, -is, *f.,* steep cliff, crag

rūs, rūris, *n.,* the country (*as opposed to the city*), country estate

Rusticus, -ī, *m., proper name,* Rusticus

Sabidius, -ī *or* **-iī,** *m., proper name,* Sabidius

Sabīnus, -a, -um, *adj.,* Sabine, pertaining to the Sabines or their country

sacer, -cra, -crum, *adj.,* consecrated, sacred, hallowed

sacrilegus, -a, -um, *adj.,* sacrilegious, impious

saepe, *adv.,* often, frequently

saevus, -a, -um, *adj.,* harsh, savage, ferocious, cruel, fierce

sagum, -ī, *n.,* coarse woollen cloak or blanket

sāl, salis, *n.,* salt; wit

Sallustius, -ī *or* **-iī,** *m., proper name,* Sallustius, Sallust

saltem, *adv.,* at least, anyhow

salūbris *or* **salūber, -bris, -bre,** *adj.,* salubrious, healthful, healthy

salūs, -ūtis, *f.,* safety, well-being, health, security, refuge

salūtō (1), to greet, hail, salute, pay one's respects to

salvus, -a, -um, *adj.,* safe, secure, unharmed, intact, undamaged

sanctus, -a, -um, *adj.,* sacrosanct, inviolate, holy, sacred; virtuous, upright

sānē, *adv.,* certainly, really, decidedly, quite, yet

sapiēns, *gen.* **-ntis,** *adj.,* wise, understanding, having sound judgment

sapiō, -ere, -īvī *or* **-iī,** —, to taste of, smell of; be intelligent, show good sense

sarcina, -ae, *f.,* bundle, pack; (*pl.*) belongings

sat *or* **satis,** *adv. or indecl. noun,* enough, sufficient(ly), quite

Sāturnālicius, -a, -um, *adj.,* pertaining to Saturn

saucius, -a, -um, *adj.,* wounded, afflicted, stricken

scelerātus, -a, -um, *adj.,* accursed, heinous, criminal

scelus, -eris, *n.,* wicked act, villainy, crime

schola, -ae, *f.,* school

sciō, -īre, scīvī *or* **sciī, scītum,** to know, be aware of, be versed in

scrībō, -ere, scrīpsī, scrīptum, to inscribe, write, compose

scrīnium, -iī, *n.,* case (*for holding letters, papers, or papyrus scrolls*)

Scylla, -ae, *f., proper name,* Scylla

Scythicus, -a, -um, *adj.,* Scythian, pertaining to Scythia

sē, *acc. or abl. sing./pl. of the reflex. pron.,* himself, herself, itself, themselves

secundus, -a, -um, *adj.,* following, next, second; favorable

Secundus, -ī, *m., proper name,* Secundus

sed, *conj.,* but, however

sedeō, -ēre, sēdī, sessum, to sit, be seated, be established

Selius, -ī *or* **-iī,** *m., proper name,* Selius

semper, *adv.,* always, all the time

senecta, -ae, *f.,* old age

senex, senis, *m.,* old man; *adj.,* old, aged

sentiō, -īre, sēnsī, sēnsum, to perceive, sense, feel, discern; be alert and conscious

sepeliō, -īre, sepelīvī *or* **sepeliī, sepultum,** to inter, bury

septem, *indecl.,* seven

septingentī, -ae, -a, *pl. adj.,* seven hundred

sepulchrum, -chrī, *or* **sepulcrum, -crī,** *n.,* tomb, grave

Sertōrius, -ī or **-iī,** *m., proper name,* Sertorius

sērus, -a, -um, *adj.,* belated, slow, tardy, late

servō (1), to guard, watch, keep; preserve, save

servus, -ī, *m.,* slave

sesquipedālis, -e, *adj.,* measuring one and a half feet

sestertia, -ōrum or **-um,** *n. pl. adj. with* **mīlia** *often implied:* (so many thousand) sesterces

seu or **sīve,** *conj.,* or if; **seu . . . seu,** whether . . . or

sevēritās, -tātis, *f.,* sternness, strictness, austerity, severity

sevērus, -a, -um, *adj.,* stern, strict, austere, severe

Sextillus, -ī, *m., proper name,* Sextillus

sextus, -a, -um, *adj.,* sixth

Sextus, -ī, *m., proper name,* Sextus

sī, *conj.,* if, supposing that, in case

sīc, *adv.,* thus, so, in this way, on these terms

sīdereus, -a, -um, *adj.,* full of stars, like a star, starry, heavenly

sileō, -ēre, siluī, —, to be silent, be quiet

similis, -e, *adj.,* similar, like (+ *gen.* or *dat.*)

simplex, *gen.* **-icis,** *adj.,* simple, straightforward, plain

simplicitās, -tātis, *f.,* simplicity; frankness, candor

sine, *prep.* + *abl.,* without

sinus, -ūs, *m.,* fold of a garment, curve, bend; embrace, bosom; pocket, hollow

sitiō, -īre, —, —, to be thirsty, be parched

socer, -cerī, *m.,* father-in-law

sodālis, -is, *m.,* comrade, friend

soleō, -ēre, solitus sum, to be accustomed to, usually do, make it a practice

sollicitō (1), to disturb, harass, afflict; stimulate, rouse

sōlus, -a, -um, *adj.,* alone, lonely, sole

solūtus, -a, -um, *adj.,* unfettered, unrestrained, clear of, freed from (+ *abl.*)

solvō, -ere, solvī, solūtum, to loosen, release, relax; pay a debt

somnus, -ī, *m.,* sleep

sonō (1), to make a noise, resound

sophōs, *interj.,* bravo! well done!

sordeō, -ere, —, —, to be dirty; seem unworthy, seem not good enough

sordidus, -a, -um, *adj.,* dirty, grimy, shabby; ignominious, base

soror, -ōris, *f.,* sister

spargō, -ere, sparsī, sparsum, to scatter, sprinkle, strew, disperse

spectātor, -tōris, *m.,* witness, spectator

spectō (1), to look at, watch

spīrō (1), to breathe, be alive; give off a vapor or smell

spoliō (1), to strip, plunder,
pillage

**spondeō, -ēre, spopondī,
spōnsum,** to promise
solemnly, guarantee

spurcus, -a, -um, *adj.,* dirty,
filthy, foul, disgusting

spūtum, -ī, *n.,* spittle, spit

stāgnum, -ī, *n.,* standing water,
pool

statim, *adv.,* immediately, at
once, without delay

Stella, -ae, *m., proper name,*
Stella

Stertinius, -ī or **-iī,** *m., proper
name,* Stertinius

stertō, -ere, —, to snore

stillō (1), to drip, trickle

stō, stāre, stetī, stātum, to
stand, stand up; halt, stop

stolātus, -a, -um, *adj.,* wearing
a *stola* (*characteristic
garment of Roman matrons*)

stomachus, -ī, *n.,* stomach;
likings, taste; annoyance

stringō, -ere, strinxī, strictum,
to bind fast, secure; to bare,
unsheathe, draw (*a weapon*)

struō, -ere, struxī, structum,
to arrange, construct, build,
compose, devise

studiōsus, -a, -um, *adj.,* eager,
zealous, diligent, studious,
devoted, warmly attached

stultus, -a, -um, *adj.,* foolish,
stupid, silly

Stygius, -a, -um, *adj.,*
pertaining to the river Styx
or the underworld

sub, *prep. + acc. or abl.,* below,
beneath, under, at/to the
foot of

subdō, -ere, -didī, -ditum, to
place below or under; to
substitute

subinde, *adv.,* promptly,
thereupon; constantly,
repeatedly

subitō, *adv.,* suddenly,
unexpectedly

subitus, -a, -um, *adj.,* sudden,
without warning, hasty,
improvised

sublīmis, -e, *adj.,* high up,
elevated, lofty, eminent,
exalted

Submemmium or
Submemmius, -ī, *m./n.,
proper name,* Submemmius,
Submemmium (*see on
1.34.6*)

sufficiō, -ere, -fēcī, -fectum,
to supply, provide; be
sufficient, be adequate

sum, esse, fuī, —, to be, exist,
be present

sūmen, -inis, *n.,* sow's udder

summus, -a, -um, *adj.,* highest,
topmost; last, final

sūmō, -ere, sumpsī, sumptum,
to pick up, take

superbus, -a, -um, *adj.,* proud,
haughty, disdainful

supercilium, -iī, *n.,* eyebrow;
haughtiness, severity

supersum, -esse, -fuī, —, to
be superior; be left over,
remain

supplicium, -iī, *adj.,* propitiation, punishment, penalty

suprēmus, -a, -um, *adj.,* highest, topmost, endmost; final, last

suscitō (1), to rouse, awaken, stir to action

suspīrium, -iī, *n.,* sigh, labored breath

suspīrō (1), to sigh, draw a deep breath

susurrō (1), to speak in a low voice, whisper

suus, -a, -um, *adj.,* his, her, its, their

tabella, -ae, *f.,* board, panel; tablet, page

taberna, -ae, *f.,* booth, stall; shop, inn

taceō, -ēre, tacuī, tacitum, to be silent, keep quiet about

tālis, -e, *adj.,* of such a kind, such (*correlated with* **quālis**)

tam, *adv.,* to such a degree, so, so much

tamen, *adv.,* nevertheless, nonetheless, yet

tamquam, *conj.,* to the same degree as, just as; as if, as though

tangō, -ere, tetigī, tactum, to touch, lay hands on; affect

tantus, -a, -um, *adj.,* so great, so large, as large (*correlated with* **quantus**)

Tarpēius, -a, -um, *adj.,* pertaining to the Capitoline Hill in Rome

tectum, -ī, *n.,* roof, ceiling; house, dwelling

tegō, -ere, texī, tectum, to cover; hide, conceal

templum, -ī, *n.,* shrine, temple

tempus, -oris, *n.,* time, moment, season

tenebrae, -ārum, *f. pl.,* darkness, obscurity

tener, tenera, tenrum, *adj.,* tender, delicate, soft, sensitive

Terentius, -ī *or* **-iī,** *m., proper name,* Terentius, Terence

tergeō, -ēre, tersī, tersum, to rub clean, wipe, polish

terō, -ere, trīvī, trītum, to rub, grind; tread repeatedly

terra, -ae, *f.,* dry land, ground, region, earth

terreō, -ēre, -uī, -itum, to frighten, alarm, terrify

testis, -is, *m.,* witness; testicle

testor (1), to call as witness, affirm, testify to

thalassiō, -ōnis, *or* **Talassiō, -ōnis,** *m., ritual cry at weddings*

theātrum, -ī, *n.,* theater

Themisōn, -ōnis, *m., proper name,* Themison

thermae, -ārum, *f. pl.,* bathing establishment, baths

Thestylis, -idos *or* **-idis,** *f., proper name,* Thestylis

Thyestēs, -ae *or* **-is,** *m. proper name,* Thyestes

timeō, -ēre, -uī, —, to be afraid, fear

timidus, -a, -um, *adj.,* fearful, timid

tingō, -ere, tinxī, tinctum, to wet, soak, dye, stain

titulus, -ī, *m.,* placard, label, inscription, title

Titus, -ī, *m., proper name,* Titus

Tītyrus, -ī, *m., proper name,* Tityrus

toga, -ae, *f.,* toga

togula, -ae, *f.,* toga (*diminutive expressing contempt*)

Tonāns, -ntis, *m.,* the Thunderer (*epithet of Jupiter*)

tondeō, -ēre, —, tōnsum, to cut or clip the hair, shear, trim

Torānius, -ī *or* **-iī,** *m., proper name,* Toranius

torus, -ī, *m.,* bolster, bed (*especially the marriage-bed*)

totiēns *or* **totiēs,** *adv.,* so often, as often, so many times

tōtus, -a, -um, *adj.,* the whole of, in its entirety, all

trādō, -ere, -didī, -ditum, to hand over, deliver, surrender; relate, hand down

tremō, -ere, -uī, —, to tremble, quiver, show fright at

tremulus, -a, -um, *adj.,* trembling, shaking, quivering

trēs, tria, *adj.,* three

tribuō, -ere, -uī, -ūtum, to grant, bestow, award

tricēnsimus, -a, -um, *or* **tricēsimus, -a, -um,** *adj.,* thirtieth

tristis, -e, *adj.,* gloomy, morose, sad; stern, solemn, austere

tristitia, -ae, *f.,* unhappiness, gloom, sadness; sternness, severity, austerity

Trivia, -ae, *f., proper name,* Trivia (*epithet of Diana*)

Tryphōn, -ōnis, *m., proper name,* Tryphon

tū, *gen.* **tuī,** *pron.,* you (*sing.*)

tuba, -ae, *f.,* trumpet

Tucca, -ae, *m., proper name,* Tucca

Tullius, -ī *or* **-iī,** *m., proper name,* Tullius

Tullus, -ī, *m., proper name,* Tullus

tumidus, -a, -um, *adj.,* swollen, distended; puffed up, presumptuous

tumulus, -ī, *m.,* rounded hill, burial-mound, grave

tunica, -ae, *f.,* tunic (*basic garment of both sexes*)

turba, -ae, *f.,* disorder, turmoil; crowd, throng

turbō (1), to agitate, stir up, disturb, upset, disrupt

turpis, -e, *adj.,* offensive, ugly, shameful, disgraceful

tūs, tūris, *n.,* frankincense, incense

Tuscus, -a, -um, *adj.,* Etruscan, pertaining to Etruria or its inhabitants

tussiō, -īre, —, —, to cough

tūtus, -a, -um, *adj.,* safe, secure, sheltered

tuus, -a, -um, *adj.,* your (*sing.*)

ubi, *interr. and adv.,* where; when

ubicumque, *adv.,* in whatever place, wherever

ullus, -a, -um, *adj.,* any at all, any

ultimus, -a, -um, *adj.,* most distant, final; least important

umbra, -ae, *f.,* shadow, shade; ghost

unde, *interr. and adv.,* from where, whence; from which, and therefore

undecim, *indecl. adj.,* eleven

unguis, -is, *m.,* fingernail, toenail, claw, talon, hoof

ūnus, -a, -um, *adj.,* one, a single; one in particular; only, alone

urbs, urbis, *f.,* city, large town; Rome

ūrō, -ere, ussī, ustum, to destroy by fire, burn, scorch

ursus, -ī, *m.,* bear

usque, *adv., (with* **ad**) all the way to, right up to; *(alone)* continuously, constantly

ustus. *See* **ūrō**

ut, *conj.,* as, when; (+ *subjunctive*) in order that, even though

uter, -tra, -trum, *interr. and adj.,* which (of two)? whichever (of two)

uterque, -traque, -trumque, *pron. and adj.,* each (of two)

ūtor, -ī, ūsus sum, to use, make use of (+ *abl.*)

utrimque, *adv.,* on both sides

uxor, -ōris, *f.,* wife

Vacerra, -ae, *m., proper name,* Vacerra

vacō (1), to be empty, have room for; be available, have time for

vacuus, -a, -um, *adj.,* empty, clear, open

vagor (1), to wander, roam, move freely

vagus, -a, -um, *adj.,* roaming, wandering

valē, *imperative sing. of* **valeō,** farewell, goodbye

valeō, -ēre, -uī, -ītum, to be strong, be healthy, be well; be effective, have influence

vānus, -a, -um, *adj.,* empty, illusory; groundless, futile; fatuous, silly

vapulō (1), to be beatened, be battered

Varius, -ī *or* **-iī,** *m., proper name,* Varius

vās, vāsis, *n.,* vessel, container

vātēs, -is, *m.,* prophet, seer; poet, bard

vel, *particle,* or; possibly, even; **vel . . .vel,** either . . .or, or rather

vellō, -ere, vulsī, vulsum, to pluck, pull out

vēlox, *gen.* **-ōcis,** *adj.,* rapid, swift, speedy

Vēlox, *gen.* **-ōcis,** *m., proper name,* Velox

vēlum, -ī, *n.,* sail, awning, curtain

vēnālis, -e, *adj.,* for sale, on hire, venal

vendō, -ere, -didī, -ditum, to sell

venerābilis, -e, *adj.,* entitled to respect, august, venerable

veniō, -īre, vēnī, ventum, to come, arrive

vēnor (1), to go hunting, to hunt

venter, -tris, *m.,* belly, abdomen

Venus, -eris, *f.,* Venus *(goddess)*

verbum, -ī, *n.,* word

vērē, *adv.,* really, truly, indeed

Vergilius, -ī *or* **-iī,** *m., proper name,* Vergil, Virgil

verna, -ae, *m.,* slave born in the master's household

Vērōna, -ae, *f.,* Verona *(town in northern Italy, birthplace of Catullus)*

verrō, -ere, —, versum, to sweep clean, sweep together, sweep up

versus, -ūs, *m.,* row, line *(of verse); (pl.)* verses, poetry

vertragus, -ī, *m., name of a type of dog*

vērus, -a, -um, *adj.,* real, true, actual

vester, -tra, -trum, *adj.,* your *(pl.)*

vestiō, -īre, -īvī *or* **-iī, -ītum,** to clothe, dress, cover

vetō (1), to forbid, prohibit

vetus, *gen.* **veteris,** *adj.,* old, long-established, old-time

Vetustīna, -ae, *f., proper name,* Vetustina

via, -ae, *f.,* track, road, street; journey, way

viātor, -ōris, *m.,* traveller, wayfarer

vicārius, -iī, *m.,* substitute, deputy; slave's slave

vīcīnus, -a, -um, *adj.,* neighboring, close to

victima, -ae, *f.,* animal offered in sacrifice

victūrus, -a, -um. *See* **vīvō**

videō, -ēre, vīdī, vīsum, to see, perceive; *(pass.)* to appear, seem, be thought, be deemed

vidua, -ae, *f.,* woman who has lost her husband *(whether by death or divorce),* widow

vigilor (1), to stay awake; be watchful or vigilant

vīgintī, *indecl. adj.,* twenty

vīlicus, -ī, *m.,* overseer *(a man— slave or free—in charge of running a farm or estate)*

vincō, -ere, vīcī, victum, to conquer, defeat, beat, surpass, outdo

vindicō (1), to lay claim to; exact reparation for, punish, avenge

vīnum, -ī, *n.,* wine

vir, virī, *m.,* man *(adult male);* husband, lover

vīs, vis *(nom. pl.* **vīrēs),** force, violence; *(especially pl.)* strength, vigor

vīs, *second person sing. pres. indicative of* **volō**

viscera, -um, *n. pl.,* internal organs, innards

vispillō, -ōnis, *m.,* undertaker
(*charged with burying the
poor*)

vīta, -ae, *f.,* life

vitium, -iī, *n.,* defect, fault,
shortcoming, flaw, failing

vitrum, -ī, *n.,* glass

vīvō, -ere, vīxī, vīctum, to be
alive, live, spend one's life

vix, *adv.,* with difficulty, hardly,
scarcely, barely

vocō (1), to call, call upon,
summon, address

volitō (1), to fly, move quickly,
go to and fro

volō (1), to fly, move quickly

volō, velle, voluī, —, to want,
wish, be willing

voluptās, -tātis, *f.,* pleasure,
delight, source of joy

vorō (1), to devour, engulf

vōs, *gen.* **vestrī** *or* **vestrum,**
pron., you (*pl.*)

vōtum, -ī, *n.,* vow (*made to a
god in exchange for a favor*),
prayer, desire, hope

vox, vōcis, *f.,* voice, utterance,
word

vulnus, -eris, *n.,* wound, injury

vultus, -ūs, *m.,* facial
expression, countenance,
face, looks

Xenia, -iōrum, *n. pl.,* gifts
(*given by host to guest; the
title of a book of Martial's
epigrams*)

Zōilus, -ī, *m., proper name,*
Zoilus